PRAISE FOR

In Defense of Partisanship

"Contravening conventional wisdom, Julian Zelizer offers a spirited defense of parties and partisanship. Rather than futile attempts to reverse polarization, *In Defense of Partisanship* advocates for political and institutional reforms to channel partisan impulses toward more democratically accountable policymaking."

FRANCES LEE,
professor of politics and public affairs, Princeton University

"Julian Zelizer has long been one of America's best political historians. And this fascinating little book about the evolution of US parties and the fierce battle between them today contains more wisdom than any other volume on the subject. Anyone who cares about the past and future of our public life should read it—and politicians should take his ideas for how to reform the system to heart."

MICHAEL KAZIN,
author of *What It Took to Win: A History of the Democratic Party*, professor of history, Georgetown University

"Julian Zelizer deploys his formidable skills to illuminate what has gone wrong with American democracy and how we might fix it. *In Defense of Partisanship* is powerful and engaging, and penetrating in its analysis of how well-intentioned congressional reforms of the 1970s went so awry. Essential reading."

GARY GERSTLE,
author of *The Rise and Fall of the Neoliberal Order: America and the World in the Free Market Era*, professor of history, University of Cambridge

"How did our politics get so bad? How do we get to a better place? In this fresh, important, and wonderfully accessible book, Julian Zelizer answers the big questions with deep historical knowledge and analytical grace. It gives me hope that 'responsible partisanship' and real reform of Congress can prevail."

JONATHAN ALTER,
author of *American Reckoning: Inside Trump's Trial—and My Own*

"As anyone familiar with Julian Zelizer's books, articles, and broadcasts about American politics already knows, he is one of our foremost public intellectuals. With this book, he turns his rigorous scholarship, incisive analysis, and lucid prose to the defense of what he aptly calls 'responsible partisanship.' Rather than offer a paean to some imaginary congressional past, or a *cri de coeur* of hopelessness about the nation's present polarization, Zelizer sets forth a plausible, achievable agenda for restoring the most productive kind of party loyalty and organization. Think of this book as a manual for democracy."

SAMUEL FREEDMAN,
author of *Into the Bright Sunshine: Young Hubert Humphrey and the Fight for Civil Rights*, professor of journalism, Columbia University

"This book is instantly essential. Too many commentators bewail our hyperpartisan politics. Julian Zelizer does something much better—he explores the long and fascinating history of America's political parties, explains the current moment, and offers a road map back to sanity."

TED WIDMER,
author of *Lincoln on the Verge: Thirteen Days to Washington*

In Defense of Partisanship

COLUMBIA GLOBAL REPORTS
NEW YORK

In Defense of Partisanship

Julian E. Zelizer

United
States

© 2021 Jeffrey L. Ward

In Defense of Partisanship

Published by Columbia Global Reports
91 Claremont Avenue, Suite 515
New York, NY 10027
globalreports.columbia.edu
facebook.com/columbiaglobalreports
@columbiaGR

Library of Congress Cataloging-in-Publication Data
Names: Zelizer, Julian E., author.
Title: In defense of partisanship / Julian E. Zelizer.
Description: New York : Columbia Global Reports, 2025. | Includes bibliographical references. |
Identifiers: LCCN 2024017822 (print) | LCCN 2024017823 (ebook) | ISBN 9798987053683 (paperback) | ISBN 9798987053690 (ebook)
Subjects: LCSH: Two-party systems--United States. | Opposition (Political science)--United States. | Party affiliation--United States.
Classification: LCC JK2265 .Z45 2025 (print) | LCC JK2265 (ebook) | DDC 324.273--dc23/eng/20240802
LC record available at https://lccn.loc.gov/2024017822
LC ebook record available at https://lccn.loc.gov/2024017823

Book design by Strick&Williams
Map design by Jeffrey L. Ward
Author photograph by Zoran Jelenic

Printed in the United States of America

In memory of Morton Keller (1929–2018), Spector Professor of History at Brandeis University, whose undergraduate seminar on American political history—which started with a fascinating discussion of Everett Carll Ladd's American Political Parties *and David Broder's* The Party's Over*—helped launch a career that has centered on trying to better understand the structures of our democracy. I feel as though I have been continuing my conversation with Mickey ever since our time together in Olin-Sang.*

CONTENTS

Partisanship, What Is It Good For?

Partisanship is a dirty word in American politics. If there is one idea on which almost everyone in our divided country seems to agree, it's that the intense loyalty of Democrats and Republicans to their respective parties is a main source of our democratic ills—division, dysfunction, distrust, and disinformation. On any given day, some elected official or expert warns of Washington's toxic environment. If Neil Postman concluded in 1985 that we were amusing ourselves to death with television, the diagnosis in 2024 is that we are tearing ourselves apart through partisanship.

Capturing the zeitgeist, one classic episode of the television show *Curb Your Enthusiasm* revolved around comedian Larry David being sexually repulsed by a woman's political affiliation. After spending the entire season pursuing an actress (played by Cady Huffman) in hopes of cashing in on his wife's tenth anniversary present to let him sleep one time with another woman, David can't bring himself to have intercourse after spotting a photograph of President George W. Bush sitting on a dressing room table. "Is that Bush?" the liberal and perpetually grumpy David mumbles as they nestle on a couch kissing. "You have a picture of Bush?" he continues, quizzically looking at the picture, unlocking their lips, before letting out a nervous laugh. "You are a Republican?" David asks. "Yes, Larry, I'm a Republican," she says before he gets up to leave. The joke lands because it reflects reality. Polls have shown that interpolitical marriages have become increasingly frowned upon, more so than interreligious or interracial unions.

It's easy to see why reasonable people are anxious about the kind of mentality that lay behind the joke. When Republican zealousness culminated in a full-blown effort to overturn the 2020 presidential election, it was rational to be frightened by how far factionalism could go. It threatened to tear apart the fabric of our democracy. When Democrats and Republicans repeatedly fail to reach agreement on some of the biggest problems of our times, such as gun control, climate change, and immigration, it is fair to conclude that the immense gulf separating red from blue causes tremendous harm to real people every day. When talented legislators retire because they can no longer tolerate the venomous atmosphere on Capitol Hill, and promising young people shun a life of politics, how can one avoid concluding that partisanship is driving away the best and brightest from public service?

And it's not just that we have partisan polarization. For most of the decades since 1968, we have confronted polarization plastered on top of divided government. There have been only a few brief moments of unified party control. Under such conditions, the odds for compromise and interpartisan dealmaking over transformative presidential initiatives remain low. As one of the leading political science textbooks argued, "Congress has all too often retreated from its constitutional mandate to initiate national policy and oversee government operations. Its prerogatives are under siege from executive decision makers, federal judges, and elite opinion makers, who constantly belittle its capacities, ignore its authority, and evade its scrutiny. Lawmakers are themselves to blame for failing to address pressing policy problems, for reinforcing disdain of the institution, and for substituting partisan allegiance for independent judgment and critical thinking."

In recent years, there has been no shortage of proposals for improved governing structures for our democracy. As they have done since the founding, Americans are constantly debating the role of partisanship and factionalism, positing different alternatives for how we should deal with these forces in national life.

The model that is most antithetical to the status quo rejects the entire premise of contemporary politics. *Madisonians* assert that factionalism is inherently destructive. There is no salvation from the detrimental impact of parties once they form, according to this perspective, so the solution is to permanently constrain them through institutions. Revering the founding father James Madison, who famously articulated warnings about factionalism in the *Federalist Papers,* this school argues that the only barrier to the natural inclination to fight and divide is a constitutional design that renders decision-making inherently cumbersome. Madisonians count on the separation of powers, federalism, and bicameralism to create enough veto points to dampen partisanship through gridlock.

Nonpartisanship envisions a political system where leaders focus on what former Republican governor of Utah Jon

Huntsman Jr. has called the "common-sense majority" by promising to find universal solutions to national problems that command widespread support. Proponents like former New York City mayor Michael Bloomberg have also called for procedural changes, such as removing party labels from ballots and eliminating primaries in municipal elections to empower unaffiliated candidates. In a nod to the Progressive Era (early 1900s), nonpartisanship assumes that technocratic elites have the capacity to design the most effective solutions to our problems with an eye trained on expert data rather than short-term political imperatives. This dream of nonpartisanship is deeply rooted in a national political culture that has perpetually wrestled with its own nature. As *New York Times* columnist Jamelle Bouie argued, "You can find this distaste for faction and longing for unity throughout American history, up to the present. Americans, including their political leadership, have a real and serious distaste for partisanship and political parties even as they are, and have been, as political and partisan a people as has ever existed."

Others believe that parties serve an important role but not as they are currently constituted. *Third-partyism* imagines a new entity that has the capacity to command broad support from the electorate and break the hold of the two major parties that have been in power since the Civil War. Third-party advocates point to polls showing how many voters identify as independent and are disaffected with the status quo; they tend to downplay the relevance of polling data that shows how most of these very citizens don't actually vote as independents but tend to support a particular party when Election Day rolls around. When this magic bullet emerges, proponents promise, the new party will offer the kind of representation that restores confidence in politics and promotes policies that have been stifled by the existing factions in our national debates.

Bipartisanship has much stronger roots in our recent history. Proponents of members cooperating across the aisle look to the decades between the 1930s and 1960s nostalgically, remembering a world of governance where a majority of politicians were eager to deliberate, negotiate, and enter into compromises. In the bipartisan world, politicians from different sides of the aisle insist on civility and nurture relationships when the workday ends. They privilege an approach to governance where elected officials are granted a fair degree of insulation from interest groups and electoral pressure to give them the space necessary to make tough and unpopular decisions. Some of the rules that ensure accountability and stifle old-fashioned politicking (such as prohibitions on earmarks) need to be jettisoned, according to this perspective, so that legislators have more chits available to broker deals. Legislation that commands support from both Democrats and Republicans, in this model, is perceived to be inherently superior and more durable than policy changes that emanate from only one party.

Another proposal for living with warring parties is to increase the power of the presidency. *Presidentialists* claim that a strong executive is essential to a functional democracy. Only presidents have the capacity to make quick, decisive, efficient, and effective decisions. As the twentieth and twenty-first centuries brought with them ongoing domestic and international crises—with the federal government playing a larger role at home and abroad—stronger centralized authority became increasingly important. New Deal and Great Society liberals turned to the executive branch (and, to some extent, the courts) to push forward policies that Congress was incapable of addressing. Meanwhile, Reaganite conservatives developed a theory of the "unitary executive" that placed the president on a pedestal high above the rest of the political system. The elevation of the president over his or her party, which accelerated under Franklin Delano Roosevelt, is perceived by this school to be a positive development. Confidence in a strong commander in chief even survived the traumatic scandals of the "Imperial Presidency" that culminated in President Richard Nixon's resignation in 1974. In a more recent book, political scientists William Howell and Terry Moe called the entire Constitution outdated, with Congress as the prime example of an institution that has outlived its expiration date, and proposed establishing a fast-track process whereby legislators could only vote presidential proposals up or down.

Although each alternative has some merit, they fail to recognize the virtues of partisanship as the best and most realistic path forward. Unfortunately, we have confused *hyperpartisanship* with *responsible partisanship*. Parties are and have been capable of producing major decisions and effectively giving representation to differences in the body politic. Gauging the value of partisanship based on the current state of affairs is to lose any sense of appreciation for how a strong two-party system constitutes the best way to organize and direct the deep tensions that always exist within the electorate while creating important connective tissue through the different decision-making points in our disjointed and fragmented political system. Barring the unlikely radical reconfiguration of our political structures into some version of a European multi-party parliamentary process, strengthening the nation's existing two-party system remains the best bet toward fostering a healthier democracy. Responsible parties have the capacity to produce significant, enduring policy results—large and small—that are perceived as legitimate among opponents.

The possibilities of responsible partisanship were at the heart of an important intellectual tradition that flourished in the 1950s and 1960s and was institutionalized through a sweeping set of congressional reforms in the 1970s and 1980s. This school of thought made a compelling case that strong, centralized, and disciplined political parties could produce (1) better policies, which reflected majoritarian opinion while granting the minority room to assert its wishes within the mainstream political process, (2) a politics that was responsive to public demands as well as differences, and (3) a government that could be held accountable to voters for the decisions that it did or did not make.

There are four reasons that achieving responsible partisanship in our own times would still contribute to the democratic process. The first is that parties have the capacity to generate bold ideas about policy and government. Robust parties, such as Democrats during the New Deal and Republicans during the Age of Reagan in the 1980s, have served as incubators for transformative proposals.

Second, competition among responsible parties can fuel legislative productivity under both united and divided government. In those rare moments when Democrats or Republicans control both branches of government, a disciplined party has often been able to produce huge breakthroughs that remake government (the New Deal, the Great Society, supply-side and deregulatory economic policy, post-9/11 national security programs, the Affordable Care Act), though the windows of opportunity close quickly. Under divided government, moreover, policymaking is possible. Indeed, even in our recent era of hyperpolarization, political scientist Jordan Tama has shown how on foreign policy bipartisanship has still driven many policy decisions. There are issues where significant blocs of one party break with the leadership, and others where both parties act in unison against leadership to check the power of the president. When the signals from the electorate are mixed, members of both parties sometimes vote together to protect their political skin. And in some cases, advocacy groups have enough muscle to overcome party leaders. Strong parties have an even better chance of discerning a way to reach agreement and can afterward legitimize difficult compromises with their followers. Since responsible parties care about winning and holding power long-term and accept the obligations of governance, they are interested in finding policy solutions that will deliver them support.

The third reason that strong parties are good for American democracy is that they provide voters with real choices as to who should lead the nation. Rather than watered-down organizations that run away from serious decisions and make false promises, responsible parties provide the electorate with an opportunity to support politicians who will fight for a clearly articulated agenda as well as the tools needed to hold elected officials accountable. As John Gerring has argued, both political parties, including in periods when cross-partisan coalitions worked against them, have been able to offer voters distinct ideological visions throughout American history.

There are very real and deep fault lines in American politics over major issues such as immigration, reproductive rights, climate change, federal regulation, public health, economic policy, and, most recently, democracy itself. In many cases, there is not much common ground. In a country where there are so many issues facing the electorate on any given day, parties can organize, simplify, sort, and explain these quandaries in ways that help voters make informed choices. And in a country that is divided on fundamental questions large and small, responsible parties provide voters with a means to express their preferences at the ballot box and instill confidence that their choice of leaders will put up a vigorous fight to win. Even when voters end up on the losing side of a debate, there is value in knowing that their party took a position that reflected what its constituency desired and pursued that position as hard as possible. Responsible parties offer the best shot to legitimate defeat among their supporters.

Finally, as political scientists Steven Levitsky and Daniel Ziblatt have argued, countries with strong political parties have often performed best in stopping authoritarianism. Party leaders have acted as powerful gatekeepers, sorting through members to elevate into power and pushing out those with authoritarian inclinations. The party officials who have made these decisions seek out individuals with coalition-building potential but who also adhere to the principles of "mutual toleration"—accepting the legitimacy of the opposition—and "institutional forbearance," which has meant adhering to normative restraints on how far one can go in deploying partisan weapons. Whereas parties in the United States had until the 1960s depended on closed, smoke-filled rooms that were not very democratic, robust parties can just as easily be fashioned so that the gatekeeping role is filled by strong leaders who are held accountable by rank-and-file members.

This book reimagines what an American politics might look like going forward without indulging in nostalgia for the way things used to be. In the end, Congress must be the main engine for responsible partisanship. If the legislative branch doesn't work within our democracy, nothing else will. Although the House and Senate have been a key source of our political problems and dysfunction, it is Congress that can save us.

For this reason, congressional reform must become a top priority. Congress will always be the core arena where the nation's democratic impulses play out, the institution where the factions and interests of our polity attempt to work out compromises and discard undesirable proposals. Capitol Hill is the political body from which a new, more responsible partisanship has the possibility of being born. Creating responsible partisanship will require bold reforms, as discussed in the final chapter of this book, that enable Congress to nurture the best that parties have to offer while reining in the dangerous hyper-partisanship that has taken hold in recent decades. A new era of party-oriented reforms has the potential both to respect the deep differences that divide us and simultaneously to create a more functional arena in which two major parties compete to shape policy while still being able to govern.

How Did We Get Here?

In 1885, a young political scientist named Woodrow Wilson took the intellectual world by storm with a landmark publication extolling the virtues of strong parties. For this Johns Hopkins–trained political scientist, the kind of disciplined and centralized parties that existed in England were the best medicine for an American government that appeared unable to deal with the problems of modernity.

Yet for much of the nation's history before his publication, many prominent thinkers and leaders did not agree.

Founding Fears

The founding fathers dreaded factionalism, which they perceived to be distinct interests that chased after their own specific objectives as opposed to the common good. Many pivotal figures wrote extensively about the dangers that factionalism posed to the stability of the republic. In *Federalist 10,* James Madison argued that a "well-constructed Union" would have the ability to "break and control the violence of faction."

A faction, Madison explained, "I understand [as] a number of citizens, whether amounting to a majority or a minority of the whole, who are united and actuated by some common impulse of passion, or of interest, adverse to the rights of other citizens, or to the permanent and aggregate interests of the community."

Factional sentiment ran counter to the virtue of republicanism, a civic ideal that privileged disinterested and independent leaders who could not be corrupted. Madison believed that factions were an inherent element in modern societies and worried that majorities would act tyrannically against the rights of minorities. "In the minds of the Federalists the measure of a free government," noted the historian Gordon Wood, "had become its ability to control factions, not, as used to be thought, those of a minority, but rather those of 'an interested and overbearing majority.'" The goal of the founders was to design the government in such a way as to reduce this threat. It was also important to make a republic that was large enough to diminish the potential for any faction to dominate the rest, in contrast to conceptions of small and homogeneous republics that had been envisioned by writers such as Montesquieu.

Madison and like-minded founders thus fought to establish a representative government—as opposed to a direct democracy—around a federal structure that apportioned power to different parts of a divided polity (what he called a "compound republic"). The Constitution would also serve as an effective check against the executive branch while allowing for a federal government that was strong enough to handle its many responsibilities.

Fears of factionalism did not dissipate after the Constitutional Convention. The first president of the United

States, George Washington, blasted the "spirit of party generally" as the "worst enemy" of democracy since it tended to "distract the public councils . . . enfeeble the public administration . . . [and agitate] the community with ill-founded jealousies and false alarms." In his farewell address, Washington warned, "The alternate domination of one faction over another, sharpened by the spirit of revenge; natural to party dissension, which in different ages and countries has perpetrated the most horrid enormities . . . is to be dreaded as the great political evil."

Indeed, concerns about factionalism have remained an integral component of the nation's political culture.

Ideals were one thing. Reality was another. Factionalism manifested itself in the formation of a two-party system with competing institutions each devoted to coordinating coalitions that could win elections and pass policies. In the realm of presidential politics, the first party era (1790s–1820s) revolved around the Federalists, led by Alexander Hamilton, who championed a robust government and urban, commercial interests, while the Democratic-Republican Party, whose main proponent was Thomas Jefferson, was ambivalent about centralized power and favorable to rural areas. Madison himself, who won election to the presidency in 1808, became one of the creators of the Democratic-Republican Party and laid out a series of arguments justifying his decision as necessary to save Republicanism. Although this nascent party system, consisting primarily of fractured elites in Washington, ended with the War of 1812, as the Republicans gained dominance and the Federalists disappeared, a second party era formed by the 1820s, pitting Democrats against Whigs. "We must always have party distinctions," Senator Martin Van Buren of New York, who had helped to build New York's Democratic machine, wrote to newspaper editor Thomas Ritchie. "Political combinations between the inhabitants of the different states are unavoidable & the most natural." Van Buren envisioned the organizational potential of parties in the US system. Parties, which Alexis de Tocqueville noted were "an evil inherent in free government," cut against the individualism in American society. Although he observed in his travels to the States that parties did not debate the grand fundamentals of politics as they did in Europe: "In America the two parties agreed on the most essential points. Neither of the two had, to succeed, to destroy an ancient order or to overthrow the whole of a social structure." The third-party era started with the formation of the Republican Party in the 1850s, which resulted in the main contenders that have been with us to this day. National and state conventions had become the essential organizational mechanisms for parties as institutions. Religious, economic, and, to some extent, sectional identities in the nineteenth century were folded into party loyalty.

In the House and Senate, political parties structured their decision-making around a committee system. Although the Constitution made no mention of how Congress should organize itself, breaking up policy and oversight jurisdiction into panels, mostly temporary, was becoming the norm for the Senate by 1816 and the House a decade later. Political scientist Charles Stewart has identified four reasons why the House and Senate embraced the committee system, although the evidence admittedly remains speculative. First, some of the impetus emanated from modernization: it was simply too difficult for the chambers to deliberate as a whole on every issue that came before them. The growing demands on the federal government kept expanding the responsibilities of Congress. Breaking up the work within a growing body of legislators offered greater efficiency. Second, Kentucky's Henry Clay, during his term as Speaker that began in 1811, strengthened the role of committees and expanded their number (they more than doubled by the time he was finished in 1825), because he believed that it was in his strategic interest to coordinate with certain representatives he trusted rather than to rely on the entire House. Clay also perceived that distributing plum committee assignments—a kind of patronage—was a way for party leaders to enhance their power. Third, the desire for greater oversight over the executive branch led the House and Senate to conclude that committees were the best mechanism to achieve this goal. Finally, as the Senate and House competed for dominance within Congress, at the same time that the legislative branch competed with the president, the leaders of each chamber felt that a streamlined decision-making process provided them the best opportunity to influence final legislative outcomes.

The Civil War (1861–1865) threw the two-party system, and the democracy, into a genuine crisis. Democrats, Whigs, and Republicans had failed to prevent the sectional disintegration of the nation into violent conflict. The inability of parties to peacefully resolve the problem of slavery revealed the limitations of their institutional power. The dysfunction of the 1850s became emblematic of how decentralization and localism could overwhelm Americans' ability to confront national challenges. So, too, did physical violence, which became a regular occurrence on the floors of Congress.

Indeed, the solidification of the two-party system was never as stable as future social scientists would remember. Within the enfranchised electorate, there was considerable party fluidity throughout the nineteenth century, as recent scholarship has shown. Political identities could shift quickly, particularly before and after the Civil War. The two major parties were composed of multiple internal coalitions within a system that was organized around federalism. As a result, the rules and dates for congressional elections varied in different states until 1874. New parties formed while older ones collapsed. Furthermore, anti-partyism remained a powerful strain of American political culture.

Yet the two-party system survived, in large part because President Abraham Lincoln and the Republicans would lead the Union to victory and reconstitute the republic when the fighting ended. In his 1863 Gettysburg Address, Lincoln said, "Now we are engaged in a great civil war, testing whether that nation, or any nation so conceived and so dedicated, can long endure." From their lowest point, through Lincoln and the GOP, parties reemerged as organizations with awesome potential.

In the twelve years that followed the end of the Civil War, congressional Republicans moved the nation through Reconstruction. In a bold assertion of federal power, congressional Republicans passed a sweeping set of policies that aimed to remake the South by working with freed slaves to build robust Black social, economic, and political institutions. The Fourteenth Amendment, ratified in 1868, provided citizenship to every person born in the United States. The Fifteenth Amendment, ratified in 1870, guaranteed that the right to vote would not be denied to US citizens. With President Andrew Johnson, a member of the National Union Party, opposed to these efforts and his successor, Republican Ulysses Grant, inconsistent and tepid on this front, Congress, under the Radical Republicans such as Thaddeus Stevens, led the way.

Reconstruction, however, quickly generated a fierce backlash from white southerners who feared the end of their autonomy to deal with race. Although Reconstruction had a huge impact on the Black community, many gains were systematically dismantled by southern opponents. Though the death of Reconstruction happened gradually, the Compromise of 1877 was a vital moment. The presidential election between Republican Rutherford Hayes and Democrat Samuel Tilden did not produce a clear winner. Both parties claimed to have been victorious in South Carolina, Florida, and Louisiana. Congress created a commission to determine the vote count and concluded that the three states should go to Hayes. When Democrats threatened to block a resolution, the parties negotiated a deal that centered on ending the federal presence in the South.

Reconstruction did not outlast the contested election, but the two-party system did. Southerners depended on restoring Democratic strength to represent their regional interests in Washington. Seeking to build a dominant coalition, Republicans looked to economic and regulatory policies as a way to move beyond some of the fractures that had opened up as a result of Reconstruction.

Championing Party

With urbanization, political parties also became powerful forces in state and local government. During the second half of the nineteenth century, the "machine" came to dominate politics in most major cities, such as New York, Boston, Chicago, and Kansas City. Machines were hierarchical single-party operations that maintained tight control over jurisdictions by using patronage, taxing power, and the administration of government to secure loyalty from supporters and to intimidate opponents. The machines were less about ideology than about organization and control. They maintained a tight structure, from captains who served at the lowest level to ward heelers who oversaw them to Assembly district leaders, all the way up to the executive committee. At the very top of the pyramid were the bosses, who were among the most feared figures in cities, though often loved by constituents for their largesse.

As the nation grew accustomed to parties, influential thinkers celebrated the value of strong partisan organization. Proponents not only enthusiastically defended parties but also sought to grant their leaders an unshakable hold on decision-making in Washington and state capitals. Some looked to European parliamentary systems as models. For most of these writers, political parties constituted the best way to assert popular control within a representative government even when there was limited direct participation.

The most important text to emerge in the nineteenth century was written in the aftermath of Reconstruction by Woodrow Wilson, then teaching at Bryn Mawr College, who is considered one of America's first professional political scientists. Soon after he was an undergraduate at Princeton University, Wilson had published an article in the *International Review,* "Cabinet Government in the United States," where he began working out his ideas about how parties should function within the American system. He was deeply influenced by English journalist Walter Bagehot's ideas about the English constitution. In 1885, Wilson published the book *Congressional Government*, based on his doctoral dissertation at Johns Hopkins University. In it, he made a pointed critique of America's constitutional blueprint.

Wilson believed that the constitutional structure of the government no longer worked. The separation of the executive from the legislative branch, he said, had rendered the federal government incapable of dealing with the critical problems of modernity, such as urbanization, industrialization, immigration, and war: "We have been made conscious by the rude shock of the war and by subsequent developments of policy, that there has been a vast alteration in the conditions of government; that the checks and balances which once obtained are no longer effective; and that we are really living under a constitution essentially different from that which we have been so long worshiping as our own peculiar and incomparable possession."

The problem revolved around the decentralization and fragmentation of power embedded in the Constitution, combined with a fragmented congressional committee system. Congress was extraordinarily powerful, able to continually diminish the presidency, but power within the institution was so dispersed and insular, as a result of committees, that the legislative branch did not act as the deliberative body it was meant to be. Wilson saw a basic difference between a government where a responsible parliamentary minister was in charge and a congressional government built around autonomous committees. In place of a prime minister enmeshed in the Parliament, working with cabinet officials drawn from the ranks of his colleagues, the US system depended on decisions from an inefficient, jerry-rigged process whereby presidents offered proposals that were frequently at odds with the multiple individuals who commanded power on Capitol Hill. As opposed to efficiency, America's Constitution produced chaos.

Decentralized committees fragmented power so much that it had become almost impossible to hold legislators accountable or for the institution as a whole to make difficult decisions. "We are ruled by a score and a half of 'little legislatures,'" Wilson lamented. The overwhelming influence of Congress, as it was constituted, was debilitating. The Constitution created so many checks that legislators could easily say no to the president of their own party should they so desire. "The business of the President, occasionally great," Wilson noted, "is usually not much above routine. Most of the time it is *mere* administration, mere obedience of directions from the masters of policy, the standing committees. Except insofar as his power of veto constitutes him a part of the legislature, the President might, not inconveniently, be a permanent officer; the first official of a carefully graded and impartially regulated civil service system, through whose sure series of merit-promotions the youngest clerk might rise even to the chief magistracy."

The two-party system was incapable of doing its job. The decentralized, local, and factional character of the parties had enabled them to be extremely effective at winning power in elections. But when it came to governing, the parties were unproductive and irrelevant.

Within Congress, the presence of parties was "obscure and intangible. Our parties marshal their adherents with the strictest possible discipline for the purpose of carrying elections, but their discipline is very slack and indefinite in dealing with legislation. At least there is within Congress no *visible*, and therefore no *controllable* party organization." They did not provide any sort of "bond of cohesion" to guide decision-making.

Wilson's book was at once a critique of and a defense of congressional power. Wilson claimed simultaneously that Congress asserted its influence via standing committee fiefdoms and that, as a flawed institution, it retained too much power over the president: "As at present constituted, the federal government lacks strength because its powers are divided, lacks promptness because its authorities are multiplied, lacks wieldiness because its processes are roundabout, lacks efficiency because its responsibility is indistinct and its action without competent direction."

All of these structural problems produced a fundamental leadership dilemma within American politics. "Power is nowhere concentrated," Wilson lamented; "it is rather deliberately and of set policy scattered amongst many small chiefs . . . in each of which a Standing Committee is the court-baron and its chairman lord-proprietor. These petty barons, some of them not a little powerful, but none of them within reach of the full powers of rule, may at will exercise an almost despotic sway within their own shires, and may sometimes threaten to convulse even the realm itself; but both their mutual jealousies and their brief and restricted opportunities forbid their combining, and each is very far from the office of common leader." In other words, there was no clear leader in the government, nor was there any distinct hierarchy of authority. Nobody was in charge and too many people shared power. In times of crisis, this posed an immense dilemma: "There is no one supreme, ultimate head—whether magistrate or representative body—which can decide at once and with conclusive authority what shall be done at those times when some decision there must be, and that immediately."

Wilson believed that centralized congressional leadership was essential for making decisions and enabling voters to know whom to hold accountable when power was abused. Implicit in his work was the notion that majority rule was the preferable guiding norm for democracy rather than minority rights. With strong parties, allied legislative leaders and presidents could act in unison: "*Power and strict accountability for its use* are the essential constituents of good government.... The best rulers are always those to whom great power is entrusted in such a manner as to make them feel that they will surely be abundantly honored and recompensed for a just and patriotic use of it, and to make them know that nothing can shield them from full retribution for every abuse of it."

Underlying Wilson's book was a belief in the efficacy of centralization and integration, which would be an animating ethos in this era of technocracy, expertise, and organization. Writing about the standing committees of the House, he argued, "It is this multiplicity of leaders, this many-headed leadership, which makes the organization of the House too complex to afford uninformed people and unskilled observers any easy clue to its methods of rule.... It is impossible to discover any unity or method in the disconnected and therefore unsystematic, confused, and desultory action of the House, or any common purpose in the measures which its Committees from time to time recommend." Wilson's vision applied to the world of politics the same kinds of bureaucratic managerial structures that were shaping the modern corporation.

For Wilson, the risks that the nation's democracy faced were not abstract, given what had happened in the Civil War. In Wilson's mind, moreover, Reconstruction had been another dangerous moment for the nation. His views about the deficiencies of political leadership were forged within the context of his being a southerner who expressed antipathy toward the robust federal effort to achieve racial justice after the war. In his book on American history, Wilson depicted Reconstruction—which was led by Radical Republicans in Congress who broke with President Andrew Johnson—as a subversive push crafted by renegade legislators who sought to impose stifling federal rule over southern whites: "While the war lasted the President had been master; the war ended, and Mr. Lincoln gone, Congress pushed its way to the front, and began to transmute fact into law, law into fact." In his synthetic history of the United States, Wilson would write of freed slaves' misguided expectations: "They had the easy faith, the simplicity, the idle hopes, the inexperience of children. Their masterless, homeless freedom made them the more pitiable, the more dependent, because under slavery they had been shielded, the weak and incompetent with the strong and capable; had never learned independence or the rough buffets of freedom." Whereas a powerful president had been essential to the preservation of the Republic during the Civil War, Reconstruction in his understanding revolved around a despotic and chaotic Republican Congress repudiating Presidents Johnson and Grant. Wilson depicted Radical Republicans as exploitive and corrupt, taking advantage of those they purported to help: "Their ignorance and credulity made them [freed Black slaves] easy dupes. A petty favor, a slender stipend, a trifling perquisite, a bit of poor land, a piece of money satisfied or silenced them.... They were easily taught to hate the men who had once held them in slavery, and to follow blindly the political party which had brought on the war of their emancipation." Therefore, Wilson praised the dismantling of Reconstruction for allowing the reestablishment of white rule. Though his writing about Congress in 1885 was crafted around a theoretical understanding of institutions, not far in the background lurked Wilson's strong views about what Radical Republicans on Capitol Hill had done wrong in the decade that followed the Civil War as they broke with the president.

Party discipline was the most potent medicine for the sickness afflicting the US government, according to Wilson, since it could counteract the corrosive impact of separated power. But to be effective, partisanship had to be the organizational framework for governing within the legislative branch and connecting Congress to the presidency. A muscular Speaker of the House, for example, needed to exert control over members by determining committee appointments—a key commodity in legislative politics—"in the interest of this or that policy, not covertly and on the sly, as one who does something of which he is ashamed, but openly and confidently, as one who does his duty." Without giving much detail, his solution was to import Britain's Cabinet government into the United States. He suggested that the president should select from Congress the ministers in his cabinet, and the cabinet would, in turn, be granted the authority to craft and propose legislation: "Cabinet government ... is, first of all, the simplest and most straight-forward system of party government. It gives explicit authority to that party majority which in any event will exercise its implicit powers to the top of its bent; which will snatch control if control be not given it."

While *The Atlantic* published a critical review of *Congressional Government*, highlighting Wilson's refusal to appreciate the dangers of majoritarianism, others praised the twenty-nine-year-old political scientist's ideas. In *The Nation*, Gamaliel Bradford described the work as "one of the most important books, dealing with political subjects, which have ever issued from the American press." The profound influence *Congressional Government* had on political science's theoretical models persisted throughout the twentieth century. Other books, such as James Bryce's *American Commonwealth*, Lawrence Lowell's *Essays on Government*, and Frank Goodnow's *Politics and Administration*, articulated similar themes, but Wilson's work had the greatest impact.

Ironically, by the time Wilson's book was published, the organization and partisan behavior of Congress, as well as the electorate, were changing in ways that addressed several of his concerns. The United States was becoming more strongly polarized along party lines and congressional leaders were asserting their authority over the rank and file.

Partisan competitiveness reached its zenith by the end of the 1880s. In a period when voting rates reached upward of 80 percent in presidential elections, huge crowds gathered to participate in raucous party parades, barbecues, rallies, and other public events. Voters engaged in partisan hoopla with the same verve that twentieth-century Americans would revel in sporting events and music concerts. Civics was not the only thing at work. Alcohol was a fundamental draw as was physical violence. "Cursing, drinking, sometimes fighting, getting black eyes and bloody noses . . . coming home with coat torn off and sometimes minus a hat," was all par for the course. Party newspapers were the main source for information. Textbooks taught children about the importance of parties to the democratic process. Party identification remained strong and consistent, passed down generationally through family and community. Election day was akin to a national celebration. To be sure, there were forces, most important regionalism, that cut against partisanship even at the height of its intensity.

On Capitol Hill, the "floors of Congress were awash in the most bitter and intense partisan rhetoric," wrote historian Joel Silbey. "Roll call voting echoed the inflamed rhetoric." The Republican majority that dominated politics from the 1890s until 1913, when Wilson started his term as president with a Democratic Congress, benefited from two ruthless, iron-fisted Republican Speakers of the House who worked closely with Republican presidents to achieve desired outcomes. Thomas Brackett Reed (1889–1891; 1895–1899) and Joseph Cannon (1903–1911) seized authority from the standing committees and shifted it into the Speakership. Reed, for instance, overcame a chief form of obstruction used by the minority called the "disappearing quorum," whereby legislators refused to say that they were present in the chamber in order to prevent a quorum from being reached. Unwilling to tolerate such obstruction, Reed counted each legislator who was present regardless of whether they said anything out loud. "I denounce you as the worst tyrant that ever ruled over a deliberative body," complained Missouri Democratic representative Richard Bland. Reed took control of the Rules Committee to handle the rules related to bills and the legislative schedule. Under Cannon, the Speaker gained the ability to control committee assignments, as Wilson had called for.

The Progressive Weakening of Parties

But the change was limited. Parties as institutions were weakened at the national, state, and local levels as a result of Progressive Era reforms that sought to make government more efficient, clean, and expert driven, free from the corruption that had become synonymous with machine bosses like Boss Tweed of New York's Tammany Hall. The Progressive Era marked a period roughly between the 1890s and 1920s, when a variety of reformers pushed for major changes in policy. Most reformers believed in the efficacy of a strong government, elite decision-making, and nonpartisan governing bodies. Many also held derogatory views about immigrants (seeking to "Americanize" them) and Black Americans even while pushing for programs to theoretically help them. Yet the progressives were divergent in focus and frequently in tension, reflecting an energetic transatlantic conversation of ideas. Some progressives advocated urban reforms that improved infrastructure, others wanted to ameliorate the suffering of the poor and impose controls on their lives, while others focused on national policies to regulate food safety, child labor, and trusts.

A large number of progressive activists across issue areas believed that the two major parties, as they had been constituted since the Civil War, were hurting the polity. "Party government," lamented journalist Herbert Croly, "has interfered with genuine popular government both by a mischievous, artificial and irresponsible method of representation, and by an enfeeblement of the administration in the interest of partisan subsistence." Progressive reforms attempted to rectify the situation. The Civil Service Reform Act of 1883 removed important sources of patronage from party control. In the 1890s, the US adoption of the Australian ballot, a ballot that the government printed and that voters cast in secret, took away the capacity of parties to monitor and intimidate voters. Numerous states introduced split-ticket voting. Experts played a bigger role in devising policies. Party competition over social safety-net benefits such as veterans' pensions generated a backlash against federal programs that could not be controlled by nonpartisan agents. A few states established primaries for presidential nominations as a way for voters to help pick candidates without the machine. Voter registration systems in northern cities, usually sold as measures to clean up corruption and improve efficiency, were also aimed at making the franchise more cumbersome for working-class, Catholic, and Jewish immigrants who were the bulwark of the machines. The Seventeenth Amendment (1913) ensured the direct election of senators. Voters, rather than the state party, were granted the ability to determine who served in the upper chamber.

In the years following the presidencies of William McKinley (1897–1901) and Theodore Roosevelt (1901–1909), the person in the Oval Office came to play a much bigger role in the strategies of most partisan reformers. Indeed, Woodrow Wilson's own thinking evolved. Although he never abandoned his belief in strong and disciplined parties, in *Constitutional Government in the United States* (1908), he shifted away from Britain's Cabinet model and argued that a muscular president was the best person to serve as the focus of leadership and the party, combining politics and governance in a single leader. Wilson wrote: "He can dominate his party by being spokesman for the real sentiment and purpose of the country, by giving direction to opinion, by giving the country at once the information and the statements of policy which will enable it to form its judgments alike of parties and of men." If a president could "lead the nation, his party can hardly resist him."

The institutional reforms from the Progressive Era were layered over the two-party system, however, rather than replacing it. Parties eroded and were forced to coexist with new forms of administrative government, but they survived as major institutions in American politics. Although the Progressive Era produced larger bureaucracies, an expanded executive branch, and laws constraining the influence of Democrats and Republicans, progressivism did not slay the party dragon. Some of the most potent third-party challenges in the nation's history, including the Progressive Party and the Socialist Party in the 1912 elections, failed to break the duopoly of the Democratic and Republican parties. For all the important reforms that took place from the 1880s to the 1930s, the internal workings of Congress were mostly left untouched other than the renewal of the seniority-based, decentralized committee system that reformers such as Wilson had condemned. In 1910, a progressive bipartisan coalition had led a revolt against Speaker Cannon and dispersed power back into the hands of the committee chairs. Even more so than the national parties, the southern barons emerged from the era relatively unscathed, a central part of the post-Reconstruction settlement that would have profound consequences for liberalism from the New Deal through the 1960s.

Despite all of his influence, President Franklin Roosevelt (1933–1945) wasn't able to wrest control away from committee leaders, and when he ultimately tried to unite his party around liberal principles, his efforts fell to defeat. For much of his first term, FDR's legislative prowess stemmed from the fact that, with every region devastated by the Great Depression, in several areas of the country the administration could find common ground on domestic programs like public works, federal relief, and rural development. When tensions flared with the southern Democratic committee chairs over his exercise of federal power, Roosevelt tended to give in to the demands of the Dixiecrats rather than vice versa. The southern conservatives were not scared of offending Black voters, since Jim Crow laws had disenfranchised them. This was the reason that many of the new programs that FDR signed into law, such as the Social Security Act (1935), excluded occupational categories that were predominantly filled by Black workers in the South (domestic and agricultural workers). The southern committee chairs' support came at the price of avoiding programs that might allow the federal government to affect race relations. The result was a New Deal that was constructed around racial apartheid in the Deep South, as the political scientist Ira Katznelson has argued. For the same reason, a majority of Roosevelt's New Deal programs granted state and local governments discretion in implementing and administering laws.

The 1938 midterms solidified the committee system. FDR had taken the gutsy step of inserting himself into the elections to campaign against several southern members of his own party (and one New Yorker). The president was frustrated with the state of his party in Congress. "I have always believed," he said, "and I have frequently stated, that my own party can succeed at the polls only so long as it continues to be the party of militant liberalism." The attempted purge was an open declaration of war against the southern Dixiecrats—just as was the decision by the party at the 1936 national convention to eliminate the century-old rule requiring nominees to receive two-thirds of the delegates, a firewall for southerners—Roosevelt's effort to create a more holistic Democratic Party. In a fireside chat, Roosevelt further warned, "An election cannot give the country a firm sense of direction if it has two or more national parties which merely have different names but are as alike in their principles and aims as peas in the same pod."

Most anti-FDR candidates exhorted voters to wake up to Roosevelt's dictatorial tendencies, targeting his plan to expand the size of the Supreme Court and reorganize the executive branch. They compared him to Hitler and Mussolini even as he was working to overcome congressional opposition to intervention in the European war. The possibility of the president throwing support behind an anti-lynching bill that New York senator Robert Wagner had been pushing was also on their minds. "What we have to do," North Carolina Democratic senator Josiah Bailey wrote to Virginia senator Harry Byrd, "is to preserve, if we can, the Democratic Party against his [Roosevelt's] efforts to make it the Roosevelt Party. But above this we must place the preservation of Constitutional Representative Government." During this period, fear of Roosevelt often overcame Dixiecrats' reluctance to cooperate with Republicans.

FDR and his advisors understood that the stakes of the midterms were enormous, especially after he directly intervened. "The Democratic Party is . . . engaged in a great struggle against reaction within the party as well as without the party," Secretary of the Interior Harold Ickes wrote to Texas Democratic congressman Maury Maverick, adding, "Reactionaries within the party are attempting to gain control of the party in order to destroy the party's devotion to the great liberal principles." The president agreed wholeheartedly: "We ought to have two real parties, one liberal and the other conservative." Therefore, he aimed to eliminate the southern congressional problem. At one point in the campaign, Roosevelt confronted Georgia senator Walter George at a rally in George's home state. With George sitting beside him, Roosevelt looked toward the audience and said, "The senior Senator from this State cannot possibly, in my judgment, be classified as belonging to the liberal school of thought."

The midterms were not good for the president or for his vision of a party united across the branches. Four of the five legislators whom he campaigned against were victorious. The senators returned to Washington feeling emboldened and ready for payback. Looking around Capitol Hill, Montana senator James Murray, who himself had altered his views about FDR, could not help but notice the sea change taking place among his colleagues. "There was a time when I would have bled and died for him [FDR], but in view of the way he has been acting I don't want to have any more dealings with him and I just intend to stay away from him and he can do as he pleases." Republicans enjoyed significant gains in both the House and Senate.

The conservative coalition of southern Democrats and Republicans that emerged, working through the committee system, exerted its influence on national politics for the next three decades. Opposed to any extension of federal power that would benefit Black Americans and industrial unions, the coalition acted as a roadblock to modern liberalism. It commanded such immense power that it was almost impossible for any president to subvert it. The southern committee chairs, who controlled more than half the major committees, worked closely with ranking Republicans regardless of what the president or party leaders demanded.

As FDR lost confidence in his ability to unify the party, he turned his energy instead to creating a strong executive branch disconnected from both parties in Congress. If the legislative branch would not work with him, he would work around it. In 1940, FDR ran for a third term without much interaction with other Democrats. In the coming years, Congress gradually delegated more areas of policy that had been at the center of partisan contention—such as trade—to the executive branch, where they were removed from the legislative realm and thereby muted as a fault line between Democrats and Republicans.

The fact that Democrats would retain control of Congress for almost five decades, other than two short spells (1947–1949 and 1953–1955), created incentives for cooperation across the aisle that complemented the internal structures of the chambers. In a period where the party machines were organizationally strong, most of the key incentives pushed officials toward bipartisan collaboration. For Democrats, the strong odds of maintaining control over Congress provided them with breathing space to negotiate with Republicans over legislation. Should Democrats alter bills to respond to Republican demands, there was little chance that doing so would somehow threaten their power. The Democratic majority was so large that they could afford to lose a few seats in any given year. If Democrats could obtain a Republican imprimatur on legislation, moreover, it would only strengthen their hand. The GOP, likewise, had reason to remain at the table. Their doing so would not change the outcome of future elections, either. As long as Republicans remained the "permanent minority," negotiating through the committee system afforded them the most realistic opportunity to be relevant. "When you're in the minority," Illinois congressman and future minority leader Robert Michel once said, "you've got to make up your mind: Are you going to be a player or are you just going to be a constant carping critic?" These decades experienced the highest levels of bipartisan roll calls in American history.

Yet for many liberals, "bipartisanship" became synonymous with conservative obstruction and anti-democratic, anti-majoritarian politics. Even though there were also northern bipartisan coalitions fighting for liberal legislation, the power of the conservatives felt disproportionate. Few members were as intimidated by New York senator Jacob Javits as by the tall and lanky Howard Smith, chairman of the House Rules Committee, or Senator Richard Russell from Georgia, the leader of the Southern Caucus. The coalition was the driving force behind reactionary legislation such as the Taft-Hartley Act (1947), which rolled back protections for labor. The chairmen consistently stifled civil rights proposals. Legislation was either buried in the House Rules and Senate Judiciary committees or defeated by a Senate filibuster. Indeed, the power of southern Democrats rested on the Jim Crow laws imposed after Reconstruction that undermined Black citizenship. Few equaled legislators in the coalition in wielding the weapon of anti-communism against their liberal opponents.

The bipartisan coalition became a prime target of the Civil Rights Movement. The NAACP considered congressional reform as urgent as legislation criminalizing lynching or ending segregation. "Repeated failure to obtain a two-thirds vote to shut off debate in the Senate on civil rights measures indicates that there is little hope for enactment of these bills in the Eighty-first Congress unless the Senate rules are amended to permit [cloture]," proclaimed the NAACP's assistant secretary when the Senate was considering reform in 1949. "Too often Senators have given lip service to civil rights while declining to vote for [cloture] on the plea that 'it is undemocratic to shut off debate.' If one really believes in civil rights he must be prepared to take effective and legitimate steps to transform his words into legislation.... Negroes are not in a mood to accept lip service as a substitute for performance."

Everyone involved in the battle for social justice believed that the bipartisan committee system, with its arsenal of procedures, was intertwined with the failure to pass legislation. Bipartisanship, in the estimation of most liberals, was stifling majoritarian demands. As Minnesota senator Hubert Humphrey declared in one of his maiden speeches on the floor, "The rules of the upper chamber made it possible for a determined and organized minority of Senators to keep this body from taking any action at all, by refusing to stop talking and thus preventing the Senate from voting. The coalition of Republicans and Southern Democrats being formed before us today has serious consequences for Americans. By refusing to face the need for civil rights, we have given strength to the totalitarian forces within our society from the right and the left."

APSA's 1950 Report on Responsible Partisanship

With Wilson's analytical arguments about Congress looming large in the scholarly imagination, a new generation of political scientists took up the cause of partisanship in the post–World War II period. They were all driven by a concern that democratic institutions, particularly Congress, were not equipped to deal with the problems and challenges facing the nation in the modern age. The vast expansion and modernization of the presidency and executive branch since the early twentieth century had thrown new light on the rest of the political system, raising big questions about how different components functioned and what needed to be reformed. As political scientist George Galloway (who was instrumental in legislative reforms that streamlined the committee system in 1946) quipped, Congress was an "oxcart in the age of the atom."

In 1942, V. O. Key had kicked off the conversation with *Politics, Parties, and Pressure Groups.* Key's book dissected the different functions political parties played in the nation and unpacked the ways that localism undermined party organization. Key argued that there were three different components to parties—the party in the electorate, the party in government, and party organization. He stipulated, "For government to function, the obstructions of the constitutional mechanism must be overcome, and it is the party that casts a web, at times weak, at times strong, over the dispersed organs of government and gives them a semblance of unity."

The same year Key published his landmark book, E. E. Schattschneider, a professor of government at Wesleyan University, released *Party Government*. His work offered enthusiastic arguments for the salutary impact of parties on governance. In contrast to many of his peers, Schattschneider did not see an inherent tension between the Constitution and vibrant partisanship. He boldly claimed that parties had streamlined complex government structures. In a sweeping assessment of history, he argued that the parties had "supervised or adapted themselves to the conquest of a continent, the transformation of the economic system, the absorption of the largest immigrant population in the history of the world, a series of great economic crises, and the rise of the modern administrative state." There was no question, in his mind, that parties provided the best form of decision-making and leadership: "In view of this condition the superiority of party government to government by other forms of political organization is overwhelming. . . . Party government is the democratic and liberal solution of the problem of reconciling authority and liberty, for the parties can govern without destroying liberty; they can manage interests without becoming oppressive." In his view, the two-party system moderated politics rather than inflaming passions. The majority party, inherently large, needed to hold together unwieldy coalitions through compromise and by rejecting unrealistic demands. The losing party, moreover, did not want to become a permanent minority, so they likewise had incentives to maintain as wide-ranging support as possible. Like his peers, Schattschneider was critical of Congress, where the "feebleness of party leadership" undermined its effectiveness.

The release of these two books came a few years before the sweeping victories of Britain's Labour Party in 1945, which were followed by a bold set of economic interventions, all of which inspired party-oriented social scientists. The results overseas demonstrated what strong ideologically driven parties could achieve, even if most scholars in the United States no longer looked to Cabinet government as the solution but instead sought to make the nation's existing two-party system, centered around the president, more robust.

In 1946, the same year that the Legislative Reorganization Act streamlined committees by shedding some that were no longer necessary and strengthening those that remained, the American Political Science Association (APSA) set up a sixteen-member Committee on Political Parties, under Schattschneider's direction, to take a deep dive into how these organizations could be improved. Fritz Morstein Marx of American University was the main author, though Schattschneider received most of the recognition for the final publication.

Following an intensive four-year study, the APSA committee produced a lengthy report titled *Toward a More Responsible Two-Party System*. Its findings centered on the need for parties to be "democratic, responsible, and effective." This would be a contrast to the institutions that frustrated voters and led many of them to stay away from the ballot box. The current parties were relics of the Civil War era, the committee said. Repeating the criticism that decentralization and fragmentation hampered governance, the report defined desirable "responsible partisanship" as "the party in power, developing, defining, and presenting the policy alternatives which are necessary for a true choice in reaching public decisions." This group of scholars depicted a procedural system that was bogged down by state and local machines. Parties made promises during the election season but didn't feel any sense of urgency to deliver once the task of governing began. Different factions within each party all went their own ways. The committee wanted political leaders to create an "effective party system" whereby Democrats, as well as Republicans, would be "able to bring forth programs to which they commit themselves" as a result of gaining "sufficient internal cohesion to carry out these programs."

The APSA report offered a road map to achieving responsible partisanship. The team of political scientists envisioned a system where two parties offered bona fide alternatives to voters so that the electorate would not be left with a meaningless choice between Tweedledee and Tweedledum. If the parties were incentivized to articulate genuine positions when candidates were running for office, it would then be more difficult to feed voters "unsubstantiated statements and charges."

The next element of responsible partisanship involved the implementation of procedures to enable party leaders to keep elected officials under their umbrella honest, which meant imposing discipline when it came time to vote. In Congress, for instance, responsibility would entail granting party leaders such as the Speaker and Majority Leader, rather than independent chairs, the ability to control the legislative agenda as well as the schedule. The report recommended that each party caucus meet regularly and make binding decisions about legislative policy. When members followed the caucus they should be rewarded, while those who caused problems "should expect disapproval." Turning to a sports analogy, the report argued that "a chairmanship, after all, is like the position of a quarterback on a football team. It should not be given to someone who refused to be part of the team or who might even carry the ball across the wrong goal line."

Rather than allowing the chair of the House Rules Committee to determine how a bill would be handled when it reached the floor, the party leaders needed to make that decision themselves. The House also had to reduce the number of standing committees: "The proliferation of leadership committees means that in neither house of Congress is there a body of party leaders who have the power of managing party affairs in Congress and who therefore can be held accountable for it."

Centralization would break with the precedent of decisions being made in a "dictatorial manner by individual party leaders." And committee assignments should be made based on these considerations and subject to the approval of the entire caucus.

The challenge in the Senate would be different since the chamber did not have as many formal rules or a constitutionally designated head (such as the Speaker of the House). The Senate conducted its business largely through informal norms and personal relations. For decades, as journalist William White captured in *Citadel*, a bipartisan establishment ruled. Despite the differences in how rules operated, the essence of the problem in the minds of liberal proponents of reform was the same in the Senate as in the House: a coalition of Democrats and Republicans was blocking popular legislation and disempowering a liberal majority.

Outside of Congress, APSA's report picked up on an argument that Wilson had once made, namely, that presidential candidates should be chosen by a national primary rather than the national convention. Realizing that conventions would not disappear, they instead suggested making them more representative by having them meet biennially. The total number of delegates should be smaller and elected by party voters rather than handpicked by the machine.

The committee was realistic in its understanding of the obstacles that its ideas faced, given the constitutional division of power and the staggered system of elections. Whatever was needed to win reelection, as political scientist David Mayhew argued decades later, was usually the most important determinant in driving legislative behavior as opposed to collective or national goals. Since the elections of representatives, senators, and the president didn't happen at the same time, the needs for self-preservation differed within the same party. What could be good for a senator running for reelection after six years might be very different for a candidate of the same party running for his first or second term as president.

The most eye-opening recommendation was to create a sprawling party council consisting of fifty members, with representatives chosen from the national committee, the congressional party organization, the state committees, the party governors, and other key factions. "Such a Party Council," they explained, "should consider and settle the larger problems of party management, within limits prescribed by the National Convention, propose a preliminary draft of the party platform to the National Convention; interpret the platform in relation to current problems; choose for the National Convention the group of party leaders outside the party organizations; consider and make recommendations to appropriate party organs in respect to congressional candidates; and make recommendations to the National Convention, the National Committee, or other appropriate party organs with respect to conspicuous departures from general party decisions by state or local party organizations." According to the committee's plan, party platforms would be drafted every two years and the final document should be "binding" on all party members.

They did not think that there had to be total unanimity among Democrats and Republicans. Allowing for dissension was important to healthy parties. Yet it was vital that members continued in their disagreement to think of the national interest rather than local concerns.

Schattschneider's team warned that without stronger parties, extremism would be triumphant. Writing just as Senator Joseph McCarthy was emerging on the national scene with his accusations of communist spies lurking throughout the executive branch, the scholars felt that legitimate parties were important in terms of providing voters with a place to express their grievances. If the existing parties proved unable to govern, the absence of legislation would empower radical individuals and organizations that promised illusory panaceas that played to popular fear and anger.

When APSA released its final report, receiving extensive press coverage, there was criticism from within the profession. Among the critics was Austin Ranney, a scholar at the University of Illinois, who warned that the reforms outlined could have deleterious effects. In a piece for the *American Political Science Review,* Ranney pointed out that the committee had not adequately considered why the existing party system had endured for so long, despite well-known criticism from writers such as Woodrow Wilson. "The Committee's inarticulate premise," he wrote, "that it has survived because the people have not 'understood' that responsible parties will give them the kind of government they want, would be more convincing if, having made it articulate, they had adduced some evidence to support it. The assumption that of course the people don't understand, because if they did they would demand responsible parties, is hardly borne out by the presently available evidence." Democracy could not easily withstand the impact of ideological politics. There was a virtue, Ranney said, in the constitutionally imposed division that encouraged coalition-building within each party. He turned readers back to the work of A. Lawrence Lowell, the former president of Harvard University, who argued that the fragmented parties were "appropriate to the kind of government the American people want. . . . Unified, disciplined and responsible parties are appropriate *only* to a government which seeks to locate *full* public power in the hands of popular majorities." Lowell stipulated that in the United States, people wanted "majority rule only up to a point and within very definite limits." The existing parties respected a balance between majority rule and minority rights. The assumption that majority rule was always better, he said, was suspect.

For theoreticians of interest-group pluralism, based on their understanding of what made US democratic politics resilient, the APSA report's argument struck the wrong note. Social scientists believed that pluralism was the distinctive characteristic of the nation's political system, rendering it superior to the ideologically driven regimes of the Soviet Union or parts of Western Europe. Interest groups were not a problem to be solved but a solution to the problems of industrialization and urbanization. Each segment of the economy, they argued, organized along sectoral lines and in doing so produced countervailing power to one another (with unions being the most important as a counterweight to the national corporation). In this theoretical model, the constant conflict between interest groups produced a level of stability that protected the constitutional system from the dangerous swings that had been experienced in Russia and Germany. At the center of pluralism was an agreement on the rules of the game that allowed for constructive resolutions of disagreement. "The survival of a constitutional system requires some degree of consensus on required and permissible forms and purposes of political action," David Truman argued, "and . . . the troubles of some democracies can be traced to the weakness of such consensus." According to the pluralists, the style of partisanship that the report called for would destabilize the equilibrium. In sharp contrast, the decentralized and coalitional parties that had emerged from the nineteenth century worked well within the pluralists' favored framework.

Predictably, APSA's proposals didn't sit well with real-world legislators such as Speaker Sam Rayburn or Senate Majority Leader Lyndon Johnson. Neither man was excited about an external body, whether that be a council or a binding party platform, dictating an agenda to all Democrats. Based on their experience, Rayburn and Johnson understood their primary responsibility as assisting colleagues *within* their respective chambers and constituencies. In the *Washington Star*, Jim Berryman captured the tension with a cartoon of Lyndon Johnson holding a western-style saddle in one hand that says "Majority Leadership" and standing in front of the "Senatorial Ranch" and the US Capitol. Johnson is depicted holding up his left hand toward an effete Democratic National Committee (DNC) chairman Paul Butler, who is shown wearing English riding clothes and carrying a "liberal wing" saddle. The caption reads: "You're Not Going to Ride on That Thing Around Here." Butler, a liberal who chaired the DNC from 1955 to 1960, had made centralizing his party a top priority. Rayburn and Johnson undermined Butler's efforts to create an advisory council that would coordinate decisions between national and congressional party officials.

Notwithstanding all the criticism, many political scientists were convinced by the broader claims about strong and united parties, as were print reporters and liberal politicians. Almost all of the arguments were emanating from a liberal, pro-government perspective, where the operating assumption was that majoritarian sentiment favored their agenda and that if public opinion was unleashed through congressional reforms that brought down the bipartisan coalition, their views would be triumphant.

A massive outpouring of books, scholarly articles, and opinion pieces railed against the damage that a bipartisan process, via the congressional committee system, seniority, and the conservative coalition, inflicted on the body politic. Within Congress, the Democratic Study Group (DSG), a caucus of liberals formed in 1959, became a central vehicle to lobby for reform and take on southerners by matching their procedural and tactical prowess. According to political scientist James Sundquist, the DSG was the "most elaborately organized 'party within a party' in the history of the House of Representatives."

Central to the chorus of support calling for greater partisanship was the concept of "critical elections." In an influential 1955 article, V. O. Key posited that there were watershed elections that had the capacity, through landslide results, to dramatically realign power for decades, such as those in 1896 (Republicans) and 1932 (Democrats). These game-changing elections could produce one-party dominance over a substantial stretch of time during which a united and assertive party would have the chance to push legislation. For Key and those who subsequently advanced his thesis, such as Walter Dean Burnham, critical elections demonstrated that parties were engines of bold policy change in moments of crisis. By realigning power, the formation of new and enduring partisan coalitions enabled the government to respond to emerging electoral preferences and produce policy changes to resolve problems.

If any single scholar reached a level of intellectual influence comparable to Wilson on this issue, it was James MacGregor Burns, a historian and political scientist teaching at Williams College, who in 1963 published a book that focused on the "deadlock of democracy" caused by the fact that the United States had four political parties, not two. Born in Melrose, Massachusetts, in 1918, right in the middle of President Wilson's second term, Burns had been raised in a Republican family. After attending college at Williams and serving in the Army during World War II, Burns earned his doctorate at Harvard University, where he wrote a thesis critical of the legislative process titled "Congress on Trial: The Legislative Process and the Administrative State." He was part of a larger conversation in the aftermath of the war among reform-oriented scholars who believed in the need to overhaul the legislative branch so that it could handle the problems of modernity. Burns, who unsuccessfully ran for Congress in 1958, had also written a book about Franklin Roosevelt and another on John F. Kennedy. American politics, he claimed, was becoming irrelevant to most voters as the federal government could not solve what he believed to be the two great issues of the day: "the style of life of the urban and the need for fresh and creative ventures in foreign policy."

The problem with American government was baked into the Constitution, Burns asserted. The "Madisonian Model" of bicameralism, checks and balances, and separated power, all overlayed onto the system of federalism, produced a complete and utter mess. Burns unfavorably contrasted the system to a "Jeffersonian Strategy," which was a combination of competitive party politics and strong executive leadership.

According to Burns, though the nation liked to think of partisanship as a battle between Democrats and Republicans, the "Madisonian Model" had produced four political parties in Washington: the Democratic-Presidential Party, the Democratic-Congressional Party, the Republican-Presidential Party, and the Republican-Congressional Party. The presidential parties, he argued, were composed of nationally oriented presidents who championed strong executive power and who were responsive to changing majoritarian opinion. They were internationalists and cared about the welfare of the entire nation. They supported a strong federal government. As the world changed, the leaders of the two presidential parties were the figures who tended to be most responsive to new needs. Their style of leadership privileged evolving on issues and adapting to conditions.

In contrast, the congressional parties—one Republican and one Democratic—were far more conservative and parochial. Congressional Democrats and congressional Republicans were motivated by the pressure they felt from local constituencies, which frequently meant catering to the most reactionary demands since these voters generally resided outside of the big cities. Their beliefs revolved around states' rights at home and isolationism abroad. The congressional parties were insistent on checking presidential power, which, for liberals such as Burns, was a dangerous choice, given his belief that executive leadership was the only way for government to make bold and decisive decisions, especially in times when national security was threatened. In the age of the nuclear bomb, just a few minutes could make the difference between life and death. These congressional parties generally opposed a strong federal government, at least outside of national security. Whereas the presidential parties worked with big-city lawyers, financial executives, and academics who were cosmopolitan in their outlook, congressional parties allied with parochial, conservative small-town rural leaders.

The disjointed system, he said, was a disaster: "We have often been too late, and we have been too late with too little." The old logic of incrementalism was no longer working in his estimation; "the notion of the beneficent inevitability of gradual progress is open to challenge."

In contrast to APSA's 1950 report, Burns championed a strong party system led by the president rather than a council or European-style cabinet. Burns's critique and vision embodied the feelings of an entire generation that had been deeply influenced by FDR and believed in the virtues of the presidency. Roosevelt, in their minds, had saved the nation at the depths of the economic depression and mobilized the country to fight fascism despite resistance from Congress. Rather than accepting the dysfunctional multi-party system, Burns called on politicians to create a process that allowed the victorious party to govern. The party out of power would have the ability to oppose majorities. The effort would necessitate helping voters to liberate themselves from the Madisonian paralysis of fear of the majority. "We cannot unfreeze our politics," Burns wrote, "until we unfreeze our minds." He didn't do much to address how this should work with divided government, when presidents normally didn't enjoy majorities in the House and Senate.

The book laid out a series of reforms. Burns stressed that it was important to eliminate the norm of seniority within Congress and place the entire election process under the jurisdiction of the national government rather than states and localities. Some of the changes would necessitate constitutional amendments, which he understood were difficult to achieve. Burns went so far as to support both repealing the Twenty-Second Amendment (ratified in 1951)—which prevented presidents from serving more than two terms—and mandating four-year terms in the US House of Representatives.

Burns's *Deadlock of Democracy* received favorable press attention. Writing for *Commentary* magazine, renowned Yale historian C. Van Woodward told readers that "not since Charles Beard published his *Economic Interpretation of the Constitution* fifty years ago have the framers of the Constitution had so rough a time. Unlike Beard, Mr. Burns attacks neither the motives nor the methods of the framers, but rather their often-celebrated handiwork of checks and balances." In the *New York Review of Books,* NYU sociologist Dennis Wrong argued that "*The Deadlock of Democracy* will probably have great influence. It can be compared with Samuel Lubell's *The Future of American Politics,* published in 1952. Burns tries to do for the politics of the sixties what Lubell tried to do for the fifties: define the kind of national leadership demanded by the times; draw on recent trends to outline the party realignment needed to sustain such leadership; and without surrendering to partisanship tell a popular new President what he *can* do." The popular weekly newsmagazine *Time* devoted a lengthy column to outlining the argument of the book, though it warned readers that "one of Burns's favorites, Franklin Roosevelt, tried hard to swallow up the Democratic congressional party—and got bloodied up in the attempt."

Part of the attention Burns received stemmed from the fact that his argument resonated with the mounting frustration that was being expressed by liberal politicians in Congress, such as Pennsylvania senator Joseph Clark, who delivered a blistering address on the floor calling the Senate establishment the "anti-thesis of democracy," a "self-perpetuating oligarchy" of reaction, which defended "white supremacy; a stronger devotion to property than human rights; support of the military establishment; belligerence in foreign affairs; and a determination to prevent Congressional reform." Clark published a book on this theme in 1964, provocatively titled *Congress: The Sapless Branch*. "A venturesome band of members asked Congress last week to hold a mirror up to itself and confront an image that has been producing widespread dismay, criticism, and demand for reform," noted *Newsweek* in response to some comments that Clark and Burns had made. "There was an ever-mounting chorus of criticism of the hardening arteries of Congress itself," the article went on to explain. "It came from political scientists, editorialists, and legislators themselves. And it boiled down to the charge that Congress is essentially a negative instrument; that in the 1960s, its creaky, antiquated machinery is simply not up to the challenge of the times." A year later, Missouri Democratic congressman Richard Bolling published *House Out of Order*, in which he leveled a similar critique about "autocratic" committee chairs, criticizing Mississippi Democratic congressman William Colmer for ideas that were "perhaps slightly to the left of Ivan the Terrible."

The Civil Rights Movement continued to emphasize that political reform was essential to racial justice. In August 1964, as part of Freedom Summer, a group of civil rights activists from Mississippi who called themselves the Mississippi Freedom Democratic Party (MFDP) would travel on buses to the Democratic Convention in Atlantic City, demanding to be seated instead of the all-white delegates whose power derived from the activists' disenfranchisement and racial subjugation. One of their main arguments to the Credentials Committee was the fact that they fully supported the national Democratic ticket while the "regulars" were going to endorse Republican candidate Barry Goldwater. The MFDP insisted that delegates should support the national party—which meant backing Johnson at the top of the ticket and a party platform that included civil rights—and they demanded the use of a loyalty oath as a prerequisite to being seated on the floor, a call for forcing party representatives to prove their devotion to the party. In the end, President Johnson rebuffed the MFDP by pushing through a so-called compromise that gave the Black Mississippians only two symbolic at-large seats and the promise of an integrated convention in 1968. The resolution did require all delegates to take an oath to the party, which caused most of the Mississippi regulars to leave after they had won the battle. The high-profile confrontation was another moment when the civil rights struggle elevated national party loyalty above regionalism, connecting procedural questions to the historic racial debates.

For liberal reformers, it wasn't simply the impact that bipartisan conservatism had on policies that mattered. It was the anti-democratic nature of the committee process as well. Southern legislative power was based on the racist Jim Crow laws that prevented Black Americans from voting. The entire legislative process, moreover, was closed and insular. Legislators were unaccountable to the press or public. The secretive meetings through which decisions were made, outside the public view, were highly problematic in their eyes. Legislators could vote yes or no protected by rules that made it nearly impossible for anyone to know where they stood. When legislation reached the floor, rules prevented rank-and-file members from offering amendments that clashed with what the committee chairs were comfortable with. Some committee chairs prohibited the creation of subcommittees so that they could maintain total control. Votes were frequently taken in committee and on the floor without any record. Unless observers sat in the galleries to see where members stood, a politician could take an outrageous position without facing repercussions.

As the Americans for Democratic Action (ADA), an organization created to promote anti-communist liberalism, argued in the same year that Clark published his tract:

> Since 1938 this nation has confronted a national legislative system that revels in its apathy, delights in its dilatory tactics, and flaunts its resemblance to a monstrous obstacle course. The system has torn the flesh from programs of social reform and offered a prop of power to those legislators who find comfort in the mores and customs of the 19th century. It has thwarted the will of the majority; it has frustrated the men who attempt to truly represent the voters who have chosen them.... The illness is apparent. The moribund nature of Congress in the last 25 years has demonstrated with increasing clarity the need to change the rules that now bind the United States Congress to inactivity, irresponsibility, and inefficiency. Congressional reform must be achieved if this country is to meet and solve its problems.

Legislative Lessons from the Great Society

Just as Woodrow Wilson published his works on the cusp of parties producing a surge of legislation, this cluster of books from Clark, Burns, and others came out right before one of the twentieth century's greatest bursts of legislative activity. Within a few months of Burns having complained about a deadlock of democracy, Congress started to produce transformative legislation on a daily basis. Some of the political scientists who were expert on these questions grew optimistic that the nation might finally have reached a turning point. According to the scholar Stephen Bailey, whose dissertation had won APSA's Woodrow Wilson Prize in 1952, there was a "revolution" taking place before his very eyes. Seniority, secrecy, and committees were on the ropes, along with the bipartisan coalition that depended on these processes to remain in power despite championing anti-majoritarian views.

Yet the years of productivity ended up confirming to proponents that congressional reform was desperately needed. The breathtaking speed of major legislation had depended on the most unusual set of circumstances, a configuration of forces that could not be easily replicated or counted on. The 1964 civil rights legislation, for instance, had succeeded only because there was a massive grassroots movement at the peak of its power placing huge pressure on politicians to address racial injustice. Kennedy's assassination was also important to creating a historic opportunity for LBJ to call on Congress to finish work on JFK's unfulfilled agenda, which at the time of his murder had come to include civil rights. The fact that there was a president in office at this moment with uncanny legislative skills and decades of experience on Capitol Hill was pivotal.

Most important of all, the election of 1964 brought huge liberal majorities into Congress—295 Democrats in the House and 68 in the Senate, with the regional balance shifting toward liberal northerners. Meanwhile, Republicans were reeling from the fallout of right-wing Republican Barry Goldwater's landslide defeat; now they desperately ran to the center on most domestic issues, terrified of appearing to be allied with Goldwater's rejected worldview. On issues like health care for the elderly, most in the GOP were suddenly putting forward proposals of their own and entering into agreements with the administration. The southern Democrats who had blocked almost every liberal initiative were now outnumbered. A committee chair such as Arkansan Wilbur Mills, chairman of the House Ways and Means Committee, realized that he had to go along with the party leadership. Otherwise, he would be left on the losing side of the debate, appearing weak and ineffective. Rather than stopping Medicare, as he had done for almost a decade (the *New York Times* had called him a "one-man veto on Medicare"), Mills switched course in March 1965, making himself into the architect of Medicare and Medicaid.

The Great Society legislation also demonstrated that strong partisanship did not preclude bipartisanship. In fact, these years lent support to the idea that strong parties improved the odds for dealmaking across the aisle. When the dominant party pushed a coherent and bold agenda, as LBJ and the Democrats did from 1964 to 1966, they created political incentives for the minority party to enter into alliances, as occurred with the Civil Rights Act, the Voting Rights Act, and Medicare and Medicaid—including with conservative Republicans such as Senate Minority Leader Everett Dirksen of

Illinois. The devastating Republican losses in the 1964 election brought to the table the GOP as well as a number of key southern Democratic conservatives who could read the writing on the wall that their own party leaders would no longer defer to them.

The 1966 midterms offered a final coda to this stage of the conversation about partisanship. Southern Democrats and Republicans attacked the administration's record on deficits, inflation, civil rights, and Vietnam (calling for more bombing rather than less). Republicans gained forty-seven House and three Senate seats, while the southern Democratic coalition was resuscitated. There were predictions that "an effective conservative coalition, which had been dormant for two years, would be revived when the new Congress convened January 10." The spokesperson for the conservative Americans for Constitutional Action boldly proclaimed: "This means that a coalition—and we feel that there'll be one—of Southern Democrats and Republicans will block almost any program put forward by the Great Society."

Champions of reform concluded that the two-year window of productivity offered further proof, not a negation, of the need to permanently strengthen partisanship on Capitol Hill. Not only did the chance to go big with legislation happen only when many unusual developments converged but also the window tended to shut quickly. For the next two years, before shocking the world by announcing that he would not run for reelection in March 1968, Johnson was left to expend all his energy defending domestic programs from retrenchment. Mills shifted back from his role as the architect of Medicare to the politician forcing Johnson to choose between guns (Vietnam) and butter (Great Society). "In June 1968 the Great Society," noted a historian of the period, "already badly wounded at the hands of its friends and enemies alike, lost its forward movement and its inner spirit."

As the last years of Johnson's term were bogged down in Vietnam, the situation became worse. Liberals watched the administration lean on the conservative coalition to support the effort as broader portions of the party came out against the war. It seemed as though the only politicians who still believed in the deadly mission in Southeast Asia were the same ones who had stifled progress on core domestic initiatives. Southern Democrats such as Senator Richard Russell, who unbeknownst to Americans privately expressed doubts about the war directly to the president, were publicly backing the escalation in Vietnam. The absence of strong parties, the partisans argued, was also the reason there could be an insulated "foreign policy establishment" in Washington that outlasted administrations and was unaccountable to the public. These had been the supposed wise men, "the best and the brightest," as David Halberstam famously called them, who drove the nation into a catastrophic war. "Unfortunately, the notion became permanently enshrined that such nonpolitical men had a natural right to manage the nation's foreign policy," wrote *Washington Post* columnist David Broder, who continued: "Why have they been able to maintain their control over foreign policy? Because the political parties, at critical junctures, have failed to meet their responsibilities. In none of the national elections during the whole course of the escalation and de-escalation in Vietnam were the American people given a choice of defined, coherent policies toward the struggle in Indochina. The issue was either ignored entirely or smothered in a blanket of bipartisan generalities. For six long years—between

 1964 and 1970—the leadership of both parties in Congress failed to try to bring a policy declaration on Vietnam to a vote." Broder saw responsible parties as a response to the disillusionment in the national electorate.

There was, to be sure, pushback within the political science profession, as had been the case following the release of APSA's 1950 report. From 1964 to 1969, APSA conducted another major project, called "The Study of Congress." The project generated sophisticated scholarship on the problems of the legislative branch. In this case, however, the tone was different. There was more attention to the ways that existing norms and procedures smoothed decision-making in an institution as messy as Congress (a complement to the pluralist scholarship). These scholars were carrying on an alternate reform tradition within the profession that emphasized the virtues of an internally strong Congress, modernized to fit contemporary demands, that worked within the pluralist tradition. Calling themselves the "Boys of Congress," this cohort drew on the behavioral approach to studying institutions, sometimes based in Parsonian sociology, premised on the theory that social systems endured as a result of norms constraining individual choices and maintaining stability. "Against this background of executive dominance," wrote one team of scholars, "critics of every political persuasion have found Congress relegated to a secondary level of power." The University of Rochester's Richard Fenno emphasized how these internal systems could not be overturned easily, and that was a good thing. Donald Matthews of the University of Washington explained that informal norms fostered bargaining. It was not that these scholars didn't support reform—most did—but they tended to emphasize the implicit benefits of the political status quo that commentators might not be able to appreciate.

Although their work was pathbreaking within the disciplinary field of political science, their voices did not resonate in the tumultuous atmosphere outside the academic departments of higher education. In a moment of extreme public disillusionment with what was happening in Washington, many Americans were demanding bold changes in politics—and the promise of partisanship was appealing. A growing number of politicians who cut their professional teeth in the 1960s were allying with Senator Clark. These were primarily younger Democrats, joined by a handful of Republicans (such as Illinois representative Donald Rumsfeld, who led "Rumsfeld's Raiders" in a push to replace House Minority Leader Charles Halleck with Michigan's Gerald Ford following the devastating results of the 1964 election) who prioritized institutional reform. These legislators were crucial figures since they connected the world of ideas to the world of real-world politics, where there was an expanding coalition in favor of enacting change. Writing in *Playboy* magazine in 1969, Richard Bolling tried to explain that "for a Democrat to become a chairman, he need only live long enough and get reelected often enough to outdistance his colleagues. Eventually, he'll make it, although he may have the morals of a Mafia capo or the mind of a moron—or both."

Parties offered not only an effective way to drive policy agendas but also a means of organizing and expressing opposition within the mainstream political system, something that seemed more pertinent than ever before. With so many younger Americans frustrated that neither party had offered a voice for the antiwar movement, genuine party competition would give them a place to go. In his history of the rise of the idea of a party system in the United States, published in 1969, Columbia historian Richard Hofstadter opened the book by acknowledging to readers: “I do believe that the full development of the liberal democratic state in the West required that political criticism and opposition be incarnated in one or more opposition parties, free not only to express themselves within parliamentary bodies but also to agitate and organize outside them among the electorate, and to form permanent, free, recognized oppositional structures.” He ended the work by comparing the founding period to the 1960s when “the party system is now most typically criticized not for divisiveness but for offering a superficial and false conflict to the voters, for failing to pose the ‘real’ issues with clarity and responsibility, and for blocking out dissent—in effect, for protecting the unity and harmony of civil society all too completely, for blunting and minimizing conflict at too high a cost.” Anti-partyism had been replaced by weak parties, and the deeply divided nation in the Age of Aquarius would benefit from a more robust framework for opposition.

By the time the new decade started, the arguments in favor of making Congress—and all of Washington—more partisan were well-known and circulating everywhere. Partisanship had come to be seen as an elixir to the challenges afflicting the nation. Majoritarian opinion, according to the reformers, could finally win the day in a system hitherto stacked in favor of the political minority. Wilson and his peers had been right, the reformers insisted. It was time to change the way politics worked.

Dream Fulfilled?

Few predictive book titles have gone as completely awry as the one made by the *Washington Post's* David Broder in the title of his 1972 book, *The Party's Over.* Harkening back to the 1950 APSA report, Broder warned that the nation continued to be dangerously fragmented. The political scientists had been right, he said. "We have paid a high price for the instability and weakness of our governing coalitions," he noted. "Ambitious programs have been launched, but funds to finance them withheld. Commitments made by a Congress have been vetoed or impounded by a president. No party has been able to move ahead on its own agenda for very long, and the result has been years of government by fits and starts, with a mounting backlog of unkept promises and unmet needs."

There are many ways in which Broder was on target. In the realm of the presidential nomination process, reforms put into place by Democrats after their tumultuous 1968 convention (Republicans soon followed) weakened the role of the party machine in vetting and selecting nominees. The reforms ensured that voters in binding primaries and caucuses would determine the outcome rather than party bosses holed up in smoke-filled rooms. The convention delegates would also reflect a more socially diversified range of voters. Although party elites retained more power than commentators initially predicted, there was a steady erosion of authority by elite officials that became crystal clear when real estate mogul and reality show star Donald Trump ran roughshod over the preferred candidates in the 2016 Republican nomination (and to some extent in 2008 when Barack Obama defeated Hillary Clinton for the Democratic nomination).

In retrospect, however, Broder's title feels so off the mark because it was published right before one of the most intensely partisan eras in American politics in Congress and the electorate, one that we are still in today. The intellectual push for partisan reform found a rare political opening for institutional change in the 1970s. A massive opportunity for reform had opened up unlike anything that had been experienced since the Progressive Era. The turbulence over Vietnam, race relations, and cultural norms had shattered public confidence in government institutions, a sentiment that would not fade over time. The presidency, once revered, now looked imperial. The American Congress, never loved, appeared to have been complicit in enabling presidents to make dangerous decisions about public policy and abuse their power without restraint.

For more than a decade, reformers would strike a series of major blows to the committee process, which had been a target in writings about the glaring weaknesses in the legislative system that had held back the nation. By the time this period ended, the older system would be supplanted by one where strong, centralized parties had become dominant, in many ways along the lines of what reformers had dreamed of.

The dramatic intensification of partisan polarization was a product of two factors, each related but not always directly connected: institutional reforms pushed by a Washington-based coalition that enabled party leaders to assert control over their members and major electoral shifts that sorted voters geographically along party lines. Both developments, outgrowths of the turbulent 1960s and 1970s, worked in tandem and fueled each other.

First were congressional reforms that provided party leaders with the tools and organization they needed to achieve disciplined, centralized, and aggressive decision-making by supplanting the dominance of decentralized committee chairs. The reformers were motivated to act based on the sense that the nation's democratic institutions were in crisis as a result of a war that killed more than 58,000 Americans and a presidency that ended in total disgrace. Those who were seeking to repair democracy by transforming the rules of the game believed that the time had come to institutionalize the strong partisan structures long envisioned by reformers. Most of the reformers, who tended to lean toward the left side of politics, were confident that if the legislative system was finally able to respond to majoritarian demands, those demands would support liberalism. The vulnerability that all senior politicians felt at this fraught moment—the exact kind of sentiment that political scientist Douglas Arnold argued can produce legislative action that favors general over special interests—heightened the determination of young reformers to change the system and bolstered their confidence that success was possible. A coalition that operated inside and outside of Congress led the charge. Within the House and Senate, groups such as the DSG and an informal caucus of younger liberal senators allied with a network of reform groups, such as Congress Watch, Common Cause, and smaller organizations. All those groups cooperated under an umbrella association called the Committee on Congressional Reform, to lobby, mobilize support, and communicate with members while garnering media attention for the cause.

With the focus on Capitol Hill, reformers attempted to restructure each chamber so that elected officials could work within an infrastructure that privileged centralized parties while weakening seniority, committees, and secrecy. As political scientist Eric Schickler argued, multiple objectives drove different components of the reform coalition. The changes centralized and decentralized power all at once. Some measures buttressed the standing of the rank and file by dispersing power to a greater number of legislators. Other reforms consolidated decision-making power as a means of counteracting the executive branch. Achieving efficiency and transparency was important as well. The collective product would be a jumble of procedures as well as norms that sometimes contradicted one another. Nonetheless, there was a basic coherence to the reform agenda of the period. The goal for most advocates was to rebuild a legislative system with strong and accountable parties capable of being effective within the parameters of America's constitutional system. In the minds of reformers, there was no inherent contradiction between enacting some measures that centralized authority in the hands of the party leadership and other measures that decentralized power to the party's rank and file. Indeed, the ambition was to tackle the inherent challenge to partisanship in a democratic culture: how to reconcile the need to empower leaders to make tough decisions over fragmentation without fueling autocratic tendencies. "Party discipline really means that backbenchers agree to delegate power to leaders," political scientists Frances Rosenbluth and Ian Shapiro wrote in their comparative analysis of this phenomenon, "so that they can put together platforms that will win elections and then enact them when they are in power. If the leaders fail to do that, backbenchers want to and should be able to pull the plug."

The First Wave of Reform, 1970–1973

Congressional reform did not happen in one big bang. The first wave did not directly threaten the power of the conservative coalition. Rather, reformers started to build a legislative infrastructure that could potentially be used as an alternative to seniority-based power whenever the political will came about to do so. The Legislative Reorganization Act of 1970 threw sunshine onto the process by requiring committees to make recorded votes available to the public. The act also allowed television as well as radio to cover congressional hearings as long as a majority of the committee agreed. One member could demand a recorded vote and needed twenty colleagues to support them. In an era when the "right to know" was becoming an increasingly popular reform across institutions, legislators would be required to place a green card for "yea" and a red card for "nay" into the teller's box on most votes. The act also authorized the installation of an electronic voting system for the floor of the House. Besides speed and efficiency, electronic voting would ease the path for constituencies to track the vote of every legislator, thus breaking with 180 years of precedent. Knowledge about rank-and-file behavior on legislation would no longer be monopolized by party leaders, although they would now have the capacity to use the recorded votes as a way to keep pressure on their members to remain loyal. Committee chairs also suffered a few blows from the changes that were adopted. If a chair did not file a committee report after seven days of being sent a bill, according to the new rules, a majority of the panel was granted the authority to do so themselves. The legislation improved assignments for junior legislators while providing more generous resources for the committee minority to hire adequate staff.

The next important series of reforms took place within the House Democratic Caucus one year later. A top priority for those seeking to reform parties was to weaken the norm of seniority. As long as length of service determined who moved up the committee ranks, the hands of party leaders would be tied. They didn't have much sway in which member gained a seat on a desired panel—the key commodity in legislative politics—nor could they be confident that members of the prized panels would be loyal to them. Under the direction of Phillip Burton, a fierce Democratic partisan from California, the DSG enacted rules reforms that allowed committee chairs to be chosen by criteria other than seniority. According to the rules that the caucus adopted, if at least ten Democrats challenged a nomination that had been voted on by the Committee on Committees, which since the revolt against Speaker Joseph Cannon had been the House Ways and Means Committee, then the entire caucus was required to conduct an open vote. Republicans likewise decided that they would allow for criteria other than seniority to be the basis for committee assignments. Voting would take place by secret ballot. New York Republican Barber Conable believed that the new rules would ensure committee members would "in fact [serve as] leaders and not just survivors."

Although the Senate centered around new norms as opposed to codified rules, several formal changes moved the upper chamber in a similar direction. The outlook of Senate Democrats had been shifting since the 1958 midterm elections with the influx of liberal northern legislators who were eager to have a stronger, unified, nationally focused party. There was frustration with Mike Mansfield of Montana, who had been elected as Senate Majority Leader in 1961 after Johnson resigned to become vice president. "Mansfield has acted as the Senate's servant, not its master," noted *Newsweek*. The senators desired stronger leadership from their colleague. They were more national in orientation and more eager to coordinate their positions with the agenda of Democratic presidents. In early 1971, Mansfield endorsed a plan authorizing the Democratic Policy Committee—an arm of the Majority Leader and Majority Whip—to shape the agenda for the entire party instead of relying on individual committees. Though he rejected the bolder proposals from Senators Fred Harris (D-OK) and Charles Mathias (R-MD), Mansfield released a formal statement promising that there would be future hearings looking into seniority and committees. Many Republicans were enthused as well, including some on the right who were equally frustrated with the bipartisan center. Senator Goldwater blasted seniority as "outmoded and improper for a twentieth century Congress."

If liberals were hoping to find any solace from the 1972 election, they were disappointed. President Nixon enjoyed a landslide victory against South Dakota senator George McGovern, sweeping the Electoral College with numbers almost as large as FDR's in 1936. "It was a spectacular personal victory for Richard Nixon," wrote James Reston of the *New York Times*, "ten years to the day, and almost to the hour, after his most humiliating defeat by Pat Brown in the 1962 election for the governorship of California. Beaten by John Kennedy with the narrowest of margins in the presidential election of 1960, beaten again for the control of his own state in 1962, finished with American politics by his own angry proclamation exactly a decade ago, here he is now, not only vindicated but triumphant in one of the most decisive victories in the history of American Presidential politics." Although the president would still be grappling with divided government, as Democrats retained control of Congress, liberals were deeply alarmed that Nixon would soon be making a hard-right turn. They were convinced that the president would now be able to ally with the conservative coalition to go after the Great Society, and even the New Deal. As playwright Arthur Miller reportedly warned feminist Germaine Greer, a second Nixon term would mean "the Supreme Court will be castrated, and *The New York Times* will be a single mimeographed page." After Nixon won, liberal Democrats waited anxiously to see if their worst fears would be realized.

Nixon's victory shone a bright spotlight on Congress, along with the reforms that would be needed to ensure the House and Senate were responsive to national Democratic leaders and capable of stopping the president. In January 1973, the cover of the fiftieth anniversary issue of *Time* magazine featured a photograph of Speaker Joe Cannon surrounded by members of Congress old and new. Cannon, who was on the very first cover of the magazine in 1923, offered a message for modern times. After all, the issue titled "Crisis in Congress" stated, "Some current suggestions for reform have an unmistakable whiff of Cannonism to them, notably Carl Albert's plan to exact 'loyalty oaths' from new Democratic members of the Rules Committee." The article examined the growing pressure to strengthen the legislative branch as a result of Nixon's incessant attacks: "These new demands that Congress reassert itself only dramatize how far the national legislature has fallen; those lost powers were once taken for granted as Congressional prerogatives."

Then the crisis atmosphere became explosive. Nixon was at the center of one of the biggest presidential scandals in American history, Watergate. The story started with the break-in at the Democratic National Committee headquarters in June 1972. Initial discoveries of the connections that existed between the Committee for the Reelection of the President (with the apt acronym CREEP) and the burglary fueled speculation that there was more than met the eye. A series of investigations—by special prosecutors, grand juries, Congress, and the media—produced damning information about the ways that the president had abused his power. Combined with the turmoil over Vietnam, Watergate exposed the dark underside of a system where accountability was absent and the institutions protected national leaders who did bad things.

The sense that politics had moved in dangerous directions was best captured by historian Arthur Schlesinger Jr. in his 1973 book, *The Imperial Presidency.* Schlesinger, who had written three volumes about Roosevelt and worked as an advisor to President Kennedy, admitted that he had been too quick to praise the virtues of the executive branch without perceiving the obvious dangers that emanated from an unbound commander in chief. As a historian who was closely involved in Washington politics, Schlesinger's confidence in the presidency had been shattered by the catastrophic decisions behind Vietnam and then by watching Nixon stretch the understanding of presidential power beyond anything envisioned in the Constitution. "Prolonged war in Vietnam strengthened the tendencies toward both centralization and exclusion," Schlesinger argued. "So the imperial Presidency grew at the expense of the constitutional order. Like the cowbird, it hatched its own eggs and pushed the others out of the nest. And, as it overwhelmed the traditional separation of powers in foreign affairs, it began to aspire toward an equivalent centralization of power in the domestic polity," he wrote. Although Schlesinger did not abandon his appreciation for strong presidents, he admitted in this book that the time had come to rebalance interbranch power.

Growing concerns about presidential power motivated those who had championed congressional reform. Making the legislative branch stronger, more efficient, and more accountable as an institution was the best preventive medicine against a future filled with Richard Nixons. As Leroy Rieselbach, a political scientist at Indiana University, wrote, the "need to reexamine the role of Congress is essential in the wake of Watergate. A reformed and revivified national legislature might serve to restrain the executive more effectively; if such restraints could be introduced while preserving the best features of the presidency, perhaps the policy process might truly be enhanced."

To strengthen Congress without re-creating the committee-based problems that Wilson had complained about in his classic text, centralized political parties would be essential. Inverting the presidential-centered view of partisan reform that he himself had promoted, Schlesinger now placed his faith in a different interpretation of how parties could help restrain the chief executive. In his account of the Imperial Presidency, Schlesinger argued that the decline of parties in the twentieth century, as indicated by rising levels of split-ticket voting, had been a central cause of the perils Nixon exposed. For much of the century, Schlesinger argued, parties had been the "ultimate vehicle of political expression" and "voters inherited their politics as they did their religion." Schlesinger observed that "as the parties wasted away, the Presidency stood out in solitary majesty as the central focus of political emotion, the ever more potent symbol of national community. When parties were strong and media weak, Presidents were objects of respect but not of veneration." Of course, Schlesinger was in fact more concerned about the nature of the major parties than about their continued strength, which he, like others, underestimated.

In their attempt to respond to these concerns, the House Democratic Caucus voted in 1973 to hold automatic votes at the start of each session on the nominations to be committee chairs. The decision buttressed the change made in 1971 by making the vote automatic rather than requiring ten members to initiate the process. Although the caucus rejected a proposal to always conduct the vote in secret, the final compromise still authorized a secret vote when at least 20 percent of the caucus supported doing so. This was seen as a major step away from seniority. "I'm wildly happy at what we've done," boasted Burton. "We're finally getting somewhere." Frank Evans of Colorado believed the reform would serve as a permanent "reminder to the chairmen that they are creatures of the Caucus." As political scientists studying these developments predicted, due to the reform, "*every* two years, *every* chairman would be required to run the gauntlet of the party caucus."

And the reforms that weakened congressional committees kept coming. House Democrats permanently placed the Speaker, Majority Leader, and the Majority Whip on the Committee on Committees so that they could exert a formidable influence in making assignments. The chairman of Ways and Means would no longer run the show. In March 1973, House Democrats opened all committee hearings to the public unless a majority voted to close them based on national security concerns or personal privacy matters. The caucus bolstered the Steering and Policy Committee, an arm of the party leadership that was chaired by the Speaker, by authorizing the panel to serve as a forum to make decisions about the agenda, legislation, and committee assignments. Although senior chairs such as Wilbur Mills thwarted a bold proposal from Congressman Bolling to radically alter the jurisdiction of major committees—the most effective way to remove power from top committees—the caucus did authorize the Speaker to resolve jurisdictional disputes between committees rather than relying on rules, which had traditionally been a bastion of influence for southern Democrats. During this same period, Senate Republicans regularized committee votes on who should be the ranking member, a decision that needed to be ratified by the entire party.

The synergy between reforms that attempted to strengthen centralized partisan decision-making and those that aimed to enhance Congressional power was clearest with the Congressional Budget and Impoundment Control Act of 1974. The legislation, a direct response to President Nixon's aggressive assertion of power by impounding funds, created House and Senate Budget Committees to draft concurrent budget resolutions to map out a plan for the chambers. Those resolutions would serve as a blueprint when the appropriations, authorization, and taxing committees crafted their bills. If there were discrepancies in the deliberations among the various committees, the final decisions were handled in the "reconciliation" process. Importantly, reconciliation bills could not be filibustered. The legislation also created a Congressional Budget Office to provide representatives and senators with independent budgetary expertise and that limited the use of presidential impoundment. The sense of crisis generated by Nixon had produced bipartisan support. The budget reform would be complemented by a massive increase in congressional staff and independent bodies of expertise that would help the legislative branch compete with the president.

Each step toward centralization was complemented by changes that moved in the opposite direction so that the new party leaders, unlike the old committee leaders, could be held accountable. The Subcommittee Bill of Rights in 1973 empowered subcommittee chairs by granting them more staff and requiring that they be allowed to review bills within two weeks. During the 1970s and 1980s, the House also witnessed the proliferation of specialized caucuses that formed around members with like-minded issue interests. Modeled on the DSG, for instance, the Congressional Black Caucus was formed in 1971.

Watergate and Its Aftermath

If there was any doubt as to whether the drive for reform would endure, the 1974 midterm elections seemed to answer the question. Facing the prospect of impeachment, President Nixon resigned from office on August 9 in one of the most dramatic, and traumatic, moments of American political history. The decision came after Senate Republicans decided it was no longer in their party's interest to keep defending the president. Should the House send articles of impeachment to the upper chamber, Senator Goldwater, Senate Minority Leader Hugh Scott (PA), and House Minority Leader John Rhodes (AZ) warned Nixon at a private meeting on August 7, many in the GOP would vote to remove him from office. Though there had been a few weeks where his departure appeared to have calmed the storms, President Gerald Ford reignited the fury in September by pardoning Nixon for any crimes that he might have committed. Though Ford hoped to heal the nation, his announcement had the opposite effect. The president's approval rating plummeted from 71 percent in August 1974 to 50 percent by October to 37 percent by March 1975. The pardon stirred a furious reaction across the nation, undermining Ford's standing and generating accusations that he had been part of a corrupt deal. All the more reason to distrust government, all the more reason to reform it. The pardon set the stage for the midterms, which brought large numbers of non-southern Democrats (and a few Republicans) into the House and Senate. They increased the size of the Democratic majority in the House by 43 seats, growing the majority to 291. Democrats gained 3 seats in the Senate. Not only were Democratic majorities larger, but the freshmen class represented a younger generation who believed in the need for reform and had been affected by the twin crises of Vietnam and Watergate. The average age of members of the House declined to less than fifty years for the first time since World War II.

The incoming legislators, observed House Majority Leader Tip O'Neill of Massachusetts, "hadn't come up through the state legislatures. Some of them had never run for city council and county office. Close to half of them had never campaigned for any elective office before running for Congress. Many of the new members had never rung doorbells, or driven people to the polls, or stayed late stuffing envelopes at campaign headquarters." The Class of '74, Colorado's Tim Wirth explained, had cast their first vote for JFK, came of age in the era of television, and were "improbable members of Congress." Five Republicans who had served on the House Judiciary Committee and defended Nixon lost their seats. "I didn't think that Watergate would carry this far, but it has, and there is nothing I could do about it," lamented New Jersey Republican Charles Sandman, who lost to Democrat William Hughes. "The nation's voters Tuesday savagely punished the Republican Party for the sins of Watergate, the Nixon pardon, and the hardships of the economy," noted Robert Shogan in the *Los Angeles Times*, "and left the Democrats with a large share of the burden for shaping the future." The new members were more independent from traditional political mores and determined to change the way their party conducted business. They were openly enthused about a muscular style of partisanship that was not so closely wedded to the bipartisan coalition-building machine mentality of yesteryear. This was a new generation of Democrats. Although most in the Class of 1974 had run on traditional domestic issues, they came to be known as the "Watergate Babies" because they were a driving force behind reform.

The moment of reckoning in the clash between the party reformers and the committee chairs occurred in December and

 January 1975. The House Democratic Caucus, bolstered by the incoming freshman class, took action to show that committee chairs would no longer dictate how the party handled their area of policy jurisdiction. Even before the new class was sworn into office, House Democrats voted to oust Wilbur Mills from his powerful post as chairman of Ways and Means. Although Richard Bolling had failed in his effort to strip key policies away from the committee's jurisdiction earlier in the year, scandal had finally brought Mills down. On October 7, the US Park Police had discovered Mills as one of the passengers in a speeding Lincoln Continental near the Tidal Basin. When they stopped the car, his fellow passenger, Annabel Battistella—an Argentinian woman who performed locally as a stripper named Fanne Foxe—ran out of the vehicle. Mills chased her right into the water. A local reporter was on hand to capture the event for the press. Mills apologized to his constituents, blaming his addiction to painkillers and alcoholism as a result of chronic back problems. The chairman insisted that he and Battistella were just close friends. In November, voters in the Second District of Arkansas proved forgiving and reelected him to office. The reprieve was short-lived. After Mills staggered drunk onto the stage of Foxe's first public appearance later in the month, slurring his words in front of a packed house of reporters, Democrats finally forced him to resign his chair. The ground underneath Capitol Hill shook as one of the most influential men had fallen from power.

Not content just to see Mills fall, Democrats wanted to reform the committee itself. Democrats immediately turned their attention to Ways and Means by requiring the panel to create subcommittees (which Mills had prohibited) in order to disperse power. They also removed from Ways and Means the responsibility of serving as the Committee on Committees and limiting how much business could be conducted in closed executive session. In early December, Democrats granted the Steering and Policy Committee, an arm of the Speaker and Majority Leader, the authority to make committee assignments, subject to the approval of the entire caucus in the automatic vote as the session began.

When Democrats convened in early January to be sworn in, Common Cause observed that "there is a mood of reform in the air on Capitol Hill." After voting to adopt another set of reforms, such as granting the Speaker the authority to appoint Democrats to the Rules Committee and subjecting the subcommittee chairs on the Appropriations Committee to caucus approval, the next targets were chairmen themselves. Mills's downfall had only been a taste of what was to come. The ADA predicted that "this caucus meeting will go down as the greatest reform of House rules since George Norris knocked over 'Uncle Joe' Cannon in 1911."

The younger members were in a fighting mood. With the national media covering the minutiae of these proceedings with an unusual degree of interest, the new Democrats interrogated the older chairmen based on reports that had been published by Common Cause and Congress Watch analyzing their history. For the first time in their careers, the chairmen had to justify their records.

One of the unexpected marks was the Texan Wright Patman, a fierce economic populist whom the Democratic Caucus voted out of his job as head of the Committee on Banking, Currency, and Housing and replaced with a younger, liberal, Ivy

 League–educated Wisconsin Democrat, Henry Reuss. Patman's ouster showed that the new members were out to discipline all the senior members, regardless of whether they were on the left or the right. The caucus also unseated two powerful southern conservatives, W. R. Poage of Texas and F. Edward Hébert of Louisiana. As chairman of the Agriculture Committee, Poage had been a notorious opponent of food stamps and other social safety-net programs. Although he had advocated for small farmers, liberal Democrats were unhappy with the way that he had defended agribusiness. Congressman Hébert had been chairman of the House Armed Services Committee since 1971, a traditional hawk who strongly supported high levels of defense spending. Both were kicked out of their jobs, leaving Washington observers stunned. "What do we do now?" asked one member of the Steering Committee, perhaps a reference to the ending of the classic 1972 Hollywood film *The Candidate*—when Robert Redford's politically inexperienced character pulls off a dramatic upset victory to win a Senate seat, only to ask his consultant what comes next now that he actually has power.

Ohio Democrat Wayne Hays, the chairman of the House Administration Committee, acknowledged being in "a state of shock." (Hays would be pressured by the caucus into resigning one year later after the *Washington Post* revealed that the congressman had put his mistress, Elizabeth Ray, on the public payroll by hiring her as his secretary even though she admitted that she couldn't type, file, or answer the phone.) One congressional staffer who worked for the Speaker explained, "The three chairmen being thrown out in 1975 has affected the willingness of chairmen to cooperate with the leadership. In 1973 when we voted on them, they didn't get the message.

They took the positive vote as continuing support for them. In 1975 when three were deposed, they got the message. That was important." Ralph Nader, the head of Congress Watch, announced that the decisions by the caucus had "put all committee chairmen, a number of whom consistently violate caucus rules and vote more often with the Republican majority than with the Democratic, on notice that they will be accountable to the Democratic Majority." The founder of Common Cause, John Gardner, went further, claiming that the ouster "brings the seniority system crashing down. . . . It is a signal to all other House Committee chairmen that henceforth they will be held accountable."

The House also instituted a seemingly technical modification that had huge consequences for the Speaker serving as the center of party power as opposed to decentralized committee chairs. The chamber voted to enable Speakers to refer bills to multiple committees. The decision constituted a sea change from the traditional practice that had been enshrined in the nineteenth century, which allowed the Speaker to send bills to only one committee. The existing practice had empowered the committee chairmen whose panels retained jurisdiction over the relevant area of policy. With the rules adopted in 1975, the Speaker could send an entire bill to more than one committee, assign one committee the role of being the "primary" but then schedule for it to go sequentially to a number of other panels after a specified amount of time, or send different parts of a bill to different committees. As a result, the Speaker could circumvent a chair who threatened to obstruct business. If the Speaker wanted to slow down passage of a bill that a chair supported, now he had tools to do this too.

Senators responded to the zeitgeist by further empowering party leaders as well. The Democratic Conference started subjecting all committee chairs to a secret vote at the start of every session. Under the new procedure, the Democratic Steering Committee would distribute a list of proposed committee chairs. If 20 percent of the caucus called for a vote on two nominees, it would happen within two days. Throwing sunshine onto their own deliberations, the Senate also opened committee hearings.

The most important reform in the upper chamber centered on the filibuster, the heart of bipartisan anti-majoritarian power. The tradition that emerged in the nineteenth century allowed any senator or small group of senators to tie up the business of the chamber by holding the floor through talking. The filibuster, a tool of the political minority against the majority, had been the principal weapon deployed by the conservative coalition when liberals managed to move civil rights legislation to the floor. According to rules adopted in 1917, a vote from two-thirds of the Senate was needed to achieve cloture, which was the only way to end a filibuster. For liberals and civil rights activists, eliminating the "anti-democratic" filibuster had been a key objective since World War II. When each new congressional session began, liberals such as Hubert Humphrey had proposed lowering the threshold to achieve cloture to 50 percent of the Senate based on the principle of majoritarian democracy. Until the 1970s, the filibuster was reserved primarily for high-profile legislation, particularly bills that revolved around civil rights. The Senate held only forty-nine votes to obtain cloture between 1917 and 1970. But when the tool was used, it was highly effective. A key, extremely high-profile moment in the battle for civil rights had occurred when northern Democrats persuaded Midwestern Republicans to join them to end the filibuster against the Civil Rights Act of 1964. The following year, southern Democrats failed to mount an effective filibuster against the Voting Rights Act. In both cases, the lesson for liberals was not that the filibuster no longer mattered but that without this arcane tradition, Congress could actually do its job.

Although civil rights proponents had been able to overcome the filibuster in 1964 and some liberals had filibustered against President Nixon, lowering the threshold had remained a top priority. The number of votes on cloture swelled from six in 1969–1970 to twenty in 1971–1972. Majority Whip Robert Byrd (WV) introduced a two-track system in 1972, whereby the Senate could conduct its business even if colleagues were mounting a filibuster. The hope was that this adjustment would neutralize the threat of filibusters to obstruct the business of the chamber. Liberals mobilized to put the question up for a vote in 1975. A majority vote for cloture was not in the cards. But on March 7, reformers, with the support of Vice President Nelson Rockefeller, successfully reduced the number from two-thirds of the Senate (67) to three-fifths (60). Combined with the implementation of a two-track system, the possibility of closing down southern conservatives appeared to have become easier.

The election of the former Democratic governor of Georgia, Jimmy Carter, to the presidency in 1976 gave another boost to reform. Not only did Carter support further reforms to cleanse the federal government of corruption and the abuse of power, but he had succeeded with a campaign slogan, "You Can Trust Me," that showed legislators there was serious electoral support for dealing with the sordid legacy of Watergate. "I don't have any strings on me," Carter assured voters after his victory, proclaiming that he was free from the special interest groups that normally prevented any big changes from taking place in Washington.

Inspired by the Carter presidency to believe that the time was still right to fix Washington, in 1977 the House authorized television cameras to cover floor proceedings. The goal was to shine sunlight on a process that had only been open to people who were able to obtain seats in the gallery (the Senate would follow in 1986). Tennessee Democrat Al Gore, a proponent of the measure, promised that "television will change this institution.... From this day forward, every member of this body must ask himself or herself, how many Americans are listening to the debates which are made?" Legislators agreed to limit the camera feed to show only the person speaking in the well. The rationale was to avoid embarrassing members who might forget the cameras were rolling. One year later, C-SPAN, a cable network devoted to broadcasting the House feed without journalistic commentary, was launched. Both chambers passed a sweeping ethics package that tightened disclosure laws and imposed limitations on the amount and kind of outside income that was permissible for elected officials to earn.

The tensions between the reforms empowering the rank and file and those fortifying the leadership, which were meant to create strong *and* accountable parties, proved too unwieldy. By the late 1970s, House Democrats were offering floor amendments with such great frequency that they were slowing down the business of the chamber when their own party was in control. "I don't think it makes much sense to allow our rules on roll calls in effect to be used as a filibuster," complained Wisconsin's David Obey. "That is getting a little silly. How many nights have we been here . . . for three or four or five hours, having amendment after amendment that didn't mean a damn."

Freed from much of the dominance of the bipartisan "establishment," Senators were also taking advantage of the individualistic character of their institution to make demands on their colleagues by tacking on amendments to bills, filibustering, and using dilatory tactics to obstruct the chamber. Starting in the 1970s, senators were permitted to engage in a "silent filibuster," which became the norm, meaning that they didn't have to actually hold the floor and speak. The classic images depicted in movies like *Mr. Smith Goes to Washington* became relics of a bygone era. Senators just had to announce a filibuster and the deed was done. Senate Majority Leader Robert Byrd grew extremely frustrated with where things were moving. "Lyndon Johnson was a great Majority Leader," Byrd said. "But Lyndon Johnson could not lead this Senate today as he led the Senate in his day. I do not say that with any measure of disrespect for him, but it is a different Senate." He added, "I often say when I am to fill out a form and the form says 'occupation,' I should put slave" (a curious choice of words given that Byrd had once been a member of the KKK and filibustered the Civil Rights Act of 1964, though he subsequently renounced the organization and later supported civil rights).

Practicing Partisanship

Even still, parties continued to shape the institution with greater force and vigor. After President Carter proposed a major energy package in his first year in office, the new Speaker, Tip

 O'Neill, shepherded the measure through a fractured party by circumventing traditional committees. The Speaker pulled together a forty-person ad hoc committee, chaired by Ohio Democrat Thomas "Lud" Ashley, that helped design the legislation and strong-arm the measure through the lower chamber, with O'Neill's assistance. The measure was sent to multiple committees based on the authority that the House had granted in 1975. The final legislation, a watered-down version of Carter's proposal, served as a model for how party leaders could drive deliberations without deferring to the fiefdoms that traditionally dominated Capitol Hill. "The only way to score on this play," O'Neill later recalled, "was to make an end run around the existing committees of jurisdiction, and the only way to do that was to create a whole new committee just for this bill."

In the early 1980s, the Speaker took another step to centralize power by instructing the Rules Committee to make it more difficult for members to propose floor amendments. The Rules Committee itself, under the chairmanship of Richard Bolling, had come to serve as an arm of the Speaker. Restrictive special rules clamped down on floor activity. Throughout the decade, as the House became the last bastion of Democratic strength between 1981 and 1987 (in addition to the White House, Republicans had won control of the Senate in those years), Speaker O'Neill played an especially important role in building what one scholar called a "more public speakership" by spending more time on television and devoting increased attention to public communications. Gone were the days when Speakers shunned the Sunday morning talk shows and made it extremely difficult for producers to secure interviews with them. With 168 mentions on the nightly news in 1984, O'Neill was more visible than any other member. He went so far as to appear in a cameo role playing himself on the hit prime-time NBC sitcom *Cheers*.

After O'Neill retired in 1987, Democrats elected Texan Jim Wright to be Speaker. Feeling that congressional Democrats needed to defend liberalism against President Reagan and his band of conservative troops in Congress, Wright deployed the power of the party in an even more assertive fashion than his predecessor. Without reservation, Wright set the agenda, controlled the schedule and timing of votes, strengthened the office of the Whip to gain better control of votes, and intervened in committees as they drafted legislation. Despite his friendship with Republican Minority Leader Robert Michel, Wright iced out the GOP from deliberations. Commented House Majority Leader Thomas Foley of Washington, "This is a very courageous, assertive Speaker, who is not unwilling when he identifies something he wants to do to put his reputation on the line. He likes to go out and grab the nettles."

The Speaker infuriated Republicans in 1987 when he held open the time to consider a tax increase until he could find a Democrat to switch his vote. The measure passed 206 to 205. Republicans booed and hissed as the Speaker announced that it had passed. "The House is convinced the sun rises and sets over it," quipped Republican Hank Brown of Colorado, "but this is the first time I've ever seen us readjust the sun." Others in the GOP used harsher words to describe what they called Wright's dictatorial style. The conservative firebrand Robert Walker (R-PA) informed the press that Wright was "willing to run over us. When he loses battles, instead of gracefully acknowledging defeat, he cheats." In 1993, under the leadership of Thomas Foley,

House Democrats enacted a rule that empowered Speakers to easily remove and replace members of conference committees.

During the 1980s, congressional parties refined their use of campaign money as leverage. The Watergate reforms had passed in 1974, which created a Federal Election Commission, a voluntary public finance system for presidential elections, and contribution limits, but had failed to stem the flow of private money into congressional campaigns. The Supreme Court had knocked down spending restrictions that had been in the legislation in its 1976 *Buckley v. Valeo* decision, immediately eliminating a pillar of the bill. Political action committees (PACs), which had been around since the 1930s, exploded in number and influence. From 1974 to 1984, registered PACs increased to 4,009 from 608. By the mid-1980s, PACs became a key source of campaign funds for one-third of the candidates running for the House of Representatives and approximately one-fifth for the Senate. Party leaders and committee chairs started to create leadership PACs, which they used to distribute campaign funds to loyal incumbents and challengers.

National party committees—once barely relevant when state parties were more independent—became essential. The National Republican Senatorial Committee (NRSC), the National Republican Congressional Committee (NRCC), the Democratic Senatorial Campaign Committee (DSCC), and the Democratic Congressional Campaign Committee (DCCC) all turned into major forces for raising funds and spending money on elections. Candidates knew there was literally a price to pay for crossing the party leadership. At the same time, party committees developed increasingly sophisticated tools to micro-target large contributions from specific categories of individuals and PACs based on the issues that most concerned them. Simultaneously, direct mail and phone solicitation operations allowed them to achieve much greater outreach to small contributors. In addition to money, the committees provided other types of support, such as polling services and campaign consultants.

As the arms of the parties tightened their grip on elections, the old axiom of Speaker Tip O'Neill—that all politics is local—was flipped on its head. All politics was becoming national. During congressional elections, local concerns were increasingly subsumed to issues that were being driven by the national party debate. Voters would be swayed as much, if not more, by what they thought on issues such as abortion or which party should be in power on Capitol Hill than by concerns over local bridges or road projects.

The party caucuses matured, becoming ever more effective at taking on their opponents. Senate Democrats, for example, vastly expanded their staff after losing to Republicans in the 1980 election. The Democratic Policy Committee employed a communications team. Robert Byrd, now Minority Leader since Republicans won control of the Senate on Ronald Reagan's coattails, hired a press secretary. Senate party leaders gained influence as they claimed the responsibility to negotiate unanimous consent agreements whereby both parties agreed to restrictive rules before legislation was debated. These became increasingly important as the ability of old loci of power, such as committee chairs, to control the floor weakened.

Voter Sorting

Had the demographic composition of each party remained the same, the new partisan tools put in place during the 1970s could easily have been ineffective or severely limited. As political scientist David Rohde argued, strong partisan leadership was conditional on a relatively united rank and file whose preferences were responsive to the electorate. As long as the voters within the parties remained internally divided, it proved difficult for party leaders to utilize the new tools made available through reform. "In recent years, several steps have been taken toward the goal of more responsible parties. Caucuses have been strengthened, party steering groups have been created or revitalized and control over certain committee activities has been exerted," argued one political scientist. "No doubt, these steps have fortified the parties' authority over committee activities. However, the parties' ability to assert themselves is limited by their own cohesion. It is hard to believe that party mechanisms on Capitol Hill can be strong if the parties, themselves, are incoherent at the grassroots level." Between the 1950s and 1980s, split-ticket voting as a share of ballots cast more than doubled, from 12 percent of voters in 1952 to 25 percent in 1986.

By the 1980s, however, conditions were changing in ways that vastly diminished the problem of internal electoral division and carved out more space for party leaders to flex their muscle. It turned out that voters splitting their tickets was part of a process of their shifting loyalty from one party to the other.

The second pivotal development in the transformation of congressional, as well as presidential, politics centered around the sorting of the electorate in the 1980s and 1990s, which produced two relatively internally homogeneous parties. The relationship between congressional reform and electoral changes was complex and dynamic. Numerous factors outside of congressional reforms generated the dramatic movement of voters, some of which included the white southern backlash against civil rights, cheaper transportation, economic development, and rapid suburbanization. These and other forces, which affected the daily lives of Americans more than any particular new legislative rule, were behind the push and pull of voters to different sides of the political aisle.

Yet the net result of the sorting was to produce voters and rank-and-file members who were supportive of assertive party leaders, as measured through the signals they sent their representatives and senators in elections. Those leaders used their newfound power to impose order within the caucus. The combination of strong party organization and generally united party electorates would prove explosive.

The most significant shift was that Republicans capitalized on opposition to the civil rights revolution to sweep through much of the non-metropolitan South. Southern white voters outside the cities were generally antagonistic to the liberalized civil rights positions of the national Democratic Party since 1964 and prepared to abandon long-standing partisan ties. In response, Republican leaders stepped up their attacks on policies such as affirmative action and school integration to solidify their hold on formerly Democratic communities. "Who needs Manhattan when we can get the electoral votes of eleven Southern states?" asked Kevin Phillips, an architect of the "Southern Strategy" that started when Eisenhower was in office and defined the strategic path that Richard Nixon used to win election in 1968. Some of those positions also appealed to conservative voters outside the South who remained important to the GOP. Allegedly "color-blind" ideologies in white suburbs throughout the country that legitimated residential and economic segregation lent support to increasingly hard-line positions on race.

The roughly 80–20 advantage that Democrats enjoyed over the GOP among southern white men in 1960 was approaching parity as the 1980s began. "It was a realignment of massive proportions," wrote political scientist Warren Miller, "involving a Democratic-to-Republican switch of at least three out of every ten Southern nonblack male voters." Although pockets of Democratic voters in southern states remained intact, particularly in cities, by and large the region went to the Party of Lincoln, which had morphed into the Party of Nixon and then into the Party of Reagan. In 1980, approximately 40 percent of southern white conservatives identified as Republicans. In historical perspective, this number was already quite high, given the solidly Democratic leanings of the entire region. Within eight years, the percentage reached a stunning 60 percent. And the numbers kept growing.

Republican supply-side economics and deregulatory policies resonated with legions of wealthy and middle-class suburbanites who migrated from the North to live and work in the growing suburbs and exurbs of states like Georgia and Texas. Here, too, Republicans could promote ideas that sat well with southern voters and attracted wealthy and middle-class conservatives in the North and West who were part of white flight out of the cities. Very rich voters everywhere tended to stick with the GOP even as wealthier states with cutting-edge industry veered Democratic. Outside the North, sizable numbers of voters believed that economic development was a result of low-tax, anti-union policies. The fact that military contractors and army bases were a major factor in the revitalization of a devastated region made Republican rhetoric about being "tough on defense" appealing on an economic, not just ideological, level. Moreover, voters in rural areas who were increasingly disconnected from urban or suburban life liked Republican promises to turn back the clock on the social and cultural transformations born out of the 1960s. As white southerners aligned with the GOP, liberal northeastern Republicans, uncomfortable with their party's hard-right turn, faded as a significant presence in the region.

Realizing that their older base of power in the South was thinning, Democrats moved more boldly into the party's pro-government traditions—freed from the reactionary elements that the South had preserved—bolstering their strength in the coastal states and in highly educated and populated pockets of the South and Midwest. The party's focus on new areas of social and cultural liberalism such as civil, reproductive, and immigrant rights; environmentalism; skepticism toward military conflict; and gun control was attractive to suburban, upper-middle-class, and college-educated voting-aged Americans, strengthening the party with these demographics. National Democrats sufficiently distanced themselves from thorny issues such as challenging suburban homeowner rights or tackling economic inequality, which made the party seem safe to their personal bottom line. Black and Latino Americans, moreover, came to identify Democrats after 1964 as the party that championed civil rights.

Populous states such as California and New York turned into the base of the Democratic Party. Since 1992, the Republican share of big-county votes, for example, steadily declined. Whereas both parties had been competitive in urban America through the 1980s, the numbers changed dramatically. In 1984, Reagan won one hundred of the largest counties; in 2012, Republican nominee Mitt Romney was successful in only four counties that had populations bigger than 1 million people.

Even within conservative states like Texas, Georgia, and North Carolina, solidly Democratic districts formed in the areas that surrounded universities and research centers, such as Austin and Chapel Hill. The robust economic activity of these metropolitan communities depended on a younger, secular, and educated workforce. These were the kinds of voters who were more comfortable with the Democratic embrace of social and cultural liberalism than with GOP conservatism. National Democrats also tailored their economic policies by embracing a more market-oriented ethos in an effort to win over northeastern conservatives who no longer felt comfortable in the GOP. Some observers speculated that urban life naturally promoted and reified the kinds of policies that Democrats supported among the people who lived there. Urban residents used public transit, lived in dense and diverse populations, and were more exposed to the impact of government planning and intervention (think snow removal, for example).

The data was striking. In 2004, 48 percent of voters lived in what are called "landslide counties," defined as areas where one of the presidential candidates won by 20 percentage points or more. Twenty-eight years earlier, when Carter defeated Ford, just 27 percent of voters lived in such areas.

The sorting of voters, which accelerated fivefold between 1976 and 2016, fed on itself. As different parts of the country aligned along partisan lines, many Americans were more attracted to areas that felt comfortable politically. New cultural, religious, and civic institutions that appealed to more conservative-leaning voters, as well as neighbors who looked and thought just like them, made these areas even more attractive, just as Democrats felt the same draw to the big cities and surrounding communities in areas like New York, Los Angeles, and San Francisco. As the joke on *Curb Your Enthusiasm* indicated, politics was turning into a new form of religious intolerance. Americans started joining organizations that coalesced around political viewpoints, interacting with friends and family who shared common political perspectives—both in the lived world and in how they consumed media—and they veered toward elements of popular culture that reflected their points of view.

By the close of the twentieth century, partisan politics was ascendant in the electorate and in the organization of Congress. The reforms of the 1970s had built the organizational infrastructure for centralized parties to dominate the business of legislative politics. Demographic shifts produced electoral conditions where the incentives were in place for party leaders to use their new tools. As the political scientist Larry Bartels wrote in 2000, "Partisan loyalties in the American public have rebounded significantly since the mid-1970s, especially among those who actually turn out to vote." The vast journalistic and social science literature from the 1970s and 1980s reiterating Broder's message that the parties were dead was turning out to be dead wrong. The vision of reformers from the 1950s and 1960s appeared to be coming to fruition.

To be sure, the style of partisanship that emerged was distinctively American, given that it was layered over the fragmented and decentralized constitutional system. It did not replicate parliamentary systems. There were inherent limits to how far a single party could govern with force and efficiency, given the separation of powers, bicameralism, and federalism. Unlike in parliamentary systems, party leaders in Congress, and even the dominant figures in states and localities, had limited sway over staggered candidate-centered elections. Primaries were the preferred method for nominating candidates, which undercut the hold of party leaders and staff, which in other countries have greater influence.

Moreover, as divided government became normative, moments of one-party rule were becoming limited at the national level. As James Sundquist argued, fellow political scientists who had been sympathetic to Wilson's position had "paid little attention to how the government would and should function when the president and the Senate and House majorities were not all of the same party. They could in good conscience disregard that question because intervals of divided government in their experience had been infrequent and short-lived.... [Divided government] invalidates the entire theory of party government and Presidential leadership, both elements of it." Although David Mayhew documented how divided government still had the capacity to produce a notable amount of legislation, subsequent research demonstrated that divided government nonetheless reduced the chances for presidential proposals to succeed, pushed many big issues off the agenda, and increased the number of presidential vetoes. Under united government, presidents received about three out of four votes on measures they supported. The percentage fell when power was divided. The number of bills passed that the public deemed to be vital, moreover, was almost always higher when one party controlled the White House and Congress.

Notwithstanding these limitations, partisanship, American style, was better, reformers felt, than the bipartisan morass of the previous decades. For most of them, the realities of the new Washington felt like a dream on its way to being fulfilled. The partisan era was underway.

What Went Wrong?

The partisanship envisioned by reformers in the 1970s was very different from the partisanship that has taken hold in our time. Hyperpartisanship has become a debilitating force, aggravating, in many cases, the governing difficulties that drove the push for reform in most of the twentieth century.

Rather than making Congress more effective, the perpetual, vicious clashes between Democrats and Republicans became destructive. Hyperpartisanship turned Washington, and state capitals, into dens of toxic, dysfunctional blood sport. In the first two decades of the twenty-first century, elected officials spent a great deal of their time tearing the other side apart, less interested and less able to solve the problems that the nation faced. Even when the nation was physically attacked by enemies, as on 9/11, shared tragedy proved incapable of curbing the forces that pulled us apart. As Democrats and Republicans slugged it out in front of the television cameras and on social media platforms, our nation's children tragically endured gun lockdown drills and real mass shootings, watched the climate continue to deteriorate, and struggled to survive a global pandemic where lifesaving vaccines became partisan fodder. They sat stunned as the president of the United States attempted to overturn an election that he lost—and then remained the front-runner for his party's nomination three years later. Four indictments, two federal, only seemed to make him stronger.

The Troubles with Polarization

The challenging effects of intensified polarization were becoming clear by the 1980s. The number of representatives and senators who could be identified as centrists through their roll call votes steadily declined, diminishing the odds of successful bipartisan negotiations. Members of both parties were increasingly willing to deploy tools such as the filibuster to block opponents. The filibuster morphed into a procedural weapon used as a central partisan strategy, not just a tactic by individual members or clusters of senators. No longer was it reserved for high-profile issues, as had been the case earlier in the twentieth century, and it was now even being deployed for personal vendettas. The filibuster heightened the partisan incentives for the minority to avoid negotiation and for the rank and file of the majority to give leaders greater authority so that they could organize support for cloture petitions. Without senators having to physically hold the floor while filibustering, as Mr. Smith was replaced by the Invisible Man, the mechanism became a permanent buttress for super-majoritarian requirements. There were forty-three votes on cloture in 1987–1988, compared to six in 1969–1970. The supermajority norm in the Senate created conditions where legislating became extraordinarily difficult and supermajority rules didn't achieve their stated promise. As Melissa Schwartzberg argued, the protection of political minorities did not equate with the protection of the nation's most vulnerable citizens; wealthy and powerful minorities benefit disproportionally.

Republican and Democratic leaders more frequently circumvented conference committees, which had traditionally been staffed by committee chairs and ranking members, either appointing their own loyalists or working on agreements among themselves. Civility between members, as much as social scientists could measure it, was fading fast. A series of studies confirmed the deteriorating quality of professional interaction, often measured through rhetoric, between the parties. The late Speaker Sam Rayburn's famous maxim "To get along, go along" was supplanted by an institution where Republican senator Lowell Weicker (CT) felt comfortable publicly attacking fellow Republican John Heinz (PA) as an "idiot," and where Republican congressman Robert Dornan (CA) physically accosted New York Democrat Thomas Downey on the floor. Political scientist Eric Uslaner found that 63 percent of entering freshmen said that "friendly relations were important" in 1976 compared to 37 percent four years later. Cherished norms of apprenticeship and collegial reciprocity disappeared. Threatening impeachment became more commonplace.

Polarization also increased the chances that there would be backlashes to new policies that had the potential to end or severely weaken programs. Under conditions of intense division, party leaders have strong incentives to stoke opposition within their base. "Backlash politics," writes political scientist Eric Patashnik, "allows partisan leaders to highlight the costs and unintended consequences of the other side's proposals, thereby directing attention away from the tensions or conflicts over policy priorities within their own coalitions."

The Senate confirmation process likewise became a focal point of partisan conflict. The move away from relatively predictable bipartisan confirmations had started when the Senate blocked President Lyndon Johnson's appointment of Abe Fortas to become Chief Justice in 1968, which ended in Fortas resigning in the face of a scandal. Soon after, the Senate defeated President Nixon's high court appointments, Clement Haynsworth in 1969 and G. Harrold Carswell in 1970. But the real change occurred in the 1980s, when the confirmation process started to become permanently contentious along party lines, intensifying with the defeat of conservative originalist Robert Bork's nomination to the Supreme Court in 1987 as well as that of John Tower as secretary of defense two years later. Both nominations were seen as a turning point in the hardening of party lines within the Senate. The nomination process started to take longer and final votes more frequently fell along party lines. Presidents developed a dense staff infrastructure to determine which nominees fit best into party ideology and electoral needs, interest groups formed devoted to promoting nominees who benefited one party over the other, Senate confirmation votes tended to be partisan, and the public perceived the confirmation process as an integral component of political fault lines. Republicans refused to hold hearings for more than fifty of President Clinton's judicial nominees. During George W. Bush's presidency, Senate Democrats blocked a historically high level of judicial nominees.

The toxicity of the partisanship was made easier by the fact that legislators were spending less time together in

 Washington. The Monday to Friday workweek was cut down to the "Tuesday-Thursday Club." As cheap airline tickets allowed representatives and senators to travel back and forth to their districts and states, both chambers stopped scheduling votes on the bookends of the workweek. Recesses became more numerous. The result was that the personal relationships among members thinned, which made it easier to launch attacks against one another.

The detrimental effects on Congress as a policymaking institution were notable. "Half-measures, second bests," one political scientist noted in 2014, "and just-in-time legislating are the new norm, as electoral, partisan and institutional barriers limit Congress's capacity for more than lowest common denominator deals."

But the challenges posed by partisan polarization were not insurmountable. They did not negate the benefits that robust party competition could and did produce. Nor were the congressional reforms of the 1970s the primary reason that conditions disintegrated so badly in Congress in the twenty-first century.

Asymmetric Polarization

The major problem started with the transformation in the character of one of the two major parties—the GOP. Partisanship was one thing; radical partisanship another. In the crisis posed by Watergate, a new generation of younger Republicans emerged who were far more conservative in their ideas than their predecessors and much more aggressive in their partisan tactics. Sick and tired of Democratic dominance, they were determined to do whatever was necessary to rebuild after Nixon blew their opportunity to create a new majority. The lesson they took from

Senator Barry Goldwater in 1964 was not that he was wrong but, rather, that he was ahead of his time.

Using the concept of "asymmetric polarization," social scientists have documented how Democrats and Republicans polarized in different ways. The emerging cohort of congressional Republican leaders gradually embraced a style of smashmouth partisanship that abandoned most of the formal and informal guardrails that had restrained politicians in terms of how far they were willing to go to achieve victory. In addition to constituent service, being an elected official had traditionally entailed balancing three competing imperatives—partisan power, governance, and protecting democratic institutions. As the GOP attempted to build a new governing majority that would last as long as FDR's, an expanding percentage of party members was willing to jettison the second two goals in pursuit of the first. The result was an imbalance, with leaders in one major party (the GOP) feeling bound by almost no rules and the other major party (Democrats) still feeling constrained. The Republicans thus jettisoned the twin concerns that, as Steven Levitsky and Daniel Ziblatt argued, allowed them to serve as gatekeepers—mutual toleration and institutional forbearance.

Few figures were as influential in this development as Congressman Newt Gingrich of Georgia. Elected to represent the Sixth District in 1978, Gingrich replaced the retiring Dixiecrat Jack Flynt. A former moderate Republican who had supported Nelson Rockefeller and Richard Nixon in the 1960s, Gingrich inched toward the right in the mid-1970s when he perceived that the burgeoning conservative movement offered him a path to power. But his version of conservatism centered on an antiestablishment rhetoric that pitted the people against a broken Washington. Gingrich's insight was that the fallout from Vietnam and Watergate had created an electorate that was deeply distrustful of all political leaders and government institutions. After defeating Gingrich in 1974 and 1976, Flynt retired. Seizing the opportunity, Gingrich ran for the open seat in 1978 by continuing to beat the antiestablishment drum while also aligning himself with conservative positions on issues such as tax cuts, reproductive rights, and "family values." The former history professor also unleashed a brutal campaign of character assassination that tarnished his Democratic opponent Virginia Shapard's public image by portraying the moderate state legislator as a radical, anti-family, left-wing zealot. From the start of his congressional career, Gingrich rejected the emphasis on bipartisanship, civility, and good governance. Cross-party compromise, he told colleagues disapprovingly, "helps you to govern but it collapses your majority." The year that he won election, Gingrich implored a meeting of idealistic college Republicans, "This party does not need another generation of cautious, prudent, careful, bland, irrelevant, quasi-leaders who are willing as people to drift into positions because nobody else is available. What we really need are people who are tough, hard-working, energetic, willing to take risks, willing to stand up in . . . a slugfest."

Despite the conventional wisdom stipulating that Watergate would primarily hurt Republicans, Gingrich discerned how a national culture of distrust could be redirected against the Democrats. Rather than focusing entirely on the widening gulf between left and right, Gingrich positioned himself as a populist opponent of a corrupt Democratic Congress that only maintained power, he alleged, by cheating, lying, and acting in autocratic fashion. He weaponized congressional reforms from the 1970s—including sunshine laws, televised proceedings, and ethics rules—to guide his party to power after decades of wandering in the political desert as the "permanent minority." He didn't just take on the Democrats, he vilified them. Younger Republicans steeped in the "Reagan Revolution" but frustrated with the difficulty of making progress in a Democratic House were enthralled by what Gingrich was selling. Tom DeLay, a conservative former member of the Texas House of Representatives, appreciated that what Gingrich and his followers brought to the table was "a capacity for outrage that the older Republicans seemed to lack."

In 1984, Gingrich coordinated with the Conservative Opportunity Society, a small caucus he had founded a year earlier, to take advantage of the cable station C-SPAN. Every morning and at the end of each afternoon, Gingrich and others in COS, such as Robert Walker, delivered short speeches on the floor. With the chamber usually empty as legislators departed for dinner, drinks, and fundraisers, this was the time of day when any member was allowed to make a speech regardless of rank. But instead of using the speeches to flag the opening of a new post office in the district or to read from some laudatory newspaper article, as had been the tradition before the cameras were installed, members of COS took advantage of their television time to deliver blistering addresses accusing Democrats of being weak on national security and too sympathetic to communist governments in Latin America. Though C-SPAN didn't have a huge audience, Gingrich understood that he could still reach hundreds of thousands of people on any given day by appearing on the niche network.

 Since the television feed only displayed the legislator speaking, viewers watching had no way of knowing that the rest of the chamber was empty. As the Republicans asked specific Democrats to respond to their charges, it appeared to viewers as if they had nothing to say. The situation reached a boiling point when the Republicans started ripping into Massachusetts Democrat Eddie Boland, a close friend and Washington housemate of Speaker O'Neill. The Speaker was so livid at what he heard that he stepped away from the Speaker's chair and walked down to the well. Standing by the lectern, with his face blistering red, O'Neill accused Congressman Gingrich of practicing McCarthyism. The Speaker decried the Georgian's tactics: "You deliberately stood in that well before an empty House and challenged these people, and challenged their patriotism, and it is the lowest thing that I've ever seen in my thirty-two years in Congress." Gingrich, however, had the last word. Without missing a beat, the Republicans demanded that the Speaker's statement be stricken from the record based on the fact that personal insults were not permitted according to the House rules. "I move that we take the Speaker's words down," requested Mississippi Republican Trent Lott, barely able to hide the smirk on his face. The Parliamentarian sided with COS. O'Neill ended up being the person reprimanded, not Gingrich. During this conflagration, O'Neill also had ordered the cameraman to pan the chamber to show viewers that it was empty. The order violated the rules agreed on in 1978 that the cameras would show only the person speaking. Gingrich pointed to all this and more as further evidence of his claim that Democrats would do anything to win. Furthermore, Gingrich, who liked to say that you don't get on television by driving a slow car, and his fellow mavericks were pleased with the entire drama because they were being showered with national media attention. The controversy, as Gingrich expected, attracted attention. "If you get involved in a controversy, then that becomes the mesmerizing event that people remember you by," he would later explain of this method. "Don't ask me why," one television critic wrote, "but Congress is a smash hit on C-SPAN, from Podunk to Pascagoula. And suddenly Gingrich and [Robert] Walker were like Sundance Kids to millions of bored housewives, unemployed barflies and other boondock addicts." "Camscam," as it was called, gave Gingrich national stature for the first time. Never again would he recede from the public spotlight.

Five years later, Gingrich grew bolder as he took down Speaker Jim Wright based on accusations that he had violated the ethics rules that limited how much outside income a member could earn. Even before Wright had stepped into the position in January 1987, Gingrich was telling the press that Wright was the "most corrupt Speaker" in American history. He culled together a loose-leaf binder filled with newspaper and magazine articles that looked into relationships that Wright had maintained with seemingly shady constituents as well as a story about how Wright sold books to interest groups to whom he spoke (under the 1978 rules, there were limitations on how much a member could earn through honoraria but no limits on book royalties). Gingrich's ongoing attacks triggered Common Cause to call for an ethics investigation, despite having no love for or trust of Gingrich. Although the House Ethics Committee did not find in its preliminary inquiry that Wright had violated congressional rules or the law, only that there was enough justification to continue the investigation to see if solid evidence did exist, the frenzy of the scandal had grown so large that the Speaker decided to step down from his position in order to protect his party from suffering damage in the 1990 midterm elections. When the departing Speaker delivered his emotional resignation speech on the floor of the House, he implored his colleagues to stop the bloodbath. Standing in the well of the chamber, with C-SPAN broadcasting the feed, Wright explained that he was sacrificing himself to stop further political bloodshed, warning that "all of us in both political parties must resolve to bring this period of mindless cannibalism to an end! We've done enough of it!" Wright became the first Speaker in the history of the House to resign.

The "mindless cannibalism" that Wright warned of did not end. Gingrich never had any intention of slowing down. The Georgian's ultimate goal was for Republicans to reclaim control of the House for the first time since 1954. The fact that he played such a pivotal role in bringing down the Speaker only elevated his standing. His tactics appeared to work. Republicans listened attentively when Gingrich sent congressional candidates a lengthy memo through GOPAC, a Republican PAC that he controlled, urging them to abandon concerns about civility and to use blistering rhetoric to attack Democrats. His suggestions featured words such as "treasonous," "pathetic," and "anti-child." As Trent Lott recalled, "Newt was willing to tear up the system to get the majority." As a reward for his success, House Republicans had voted to place Gingrich in a leadership position in the middle of the Wright controversy, electing him as Minority Whip in 1989 (with the support of moderate Republicans such as Maine's Olympia Snowe and Nancy Johnson of Connecticut, who saw in him the only viable path to the majority). As a result, Gingrich's no-holds-barred partisanship was legitimated at the highest levels of power. Whereas Republicans censured the red-baiting Senator McCarthy for having gone too far in 1954, they rewarded Gingrich for having gone too far. As Massachusetts congressman Barney Frank quipped, "He was a kind of McCarthyite who succeeded."

After Reagan left office, Gingrich and his fellow travelers only became more frustrated when President George H. W. Bush, an old-school Republican, kept playing by the old rules of politics. His decision to enter into a deficit-reduction deal with congressional Democrats that raised taxes—despite his campaign promise, "Read My Lips: No New Taxes"—infuriated Gingrich and gave him more evidence of why radical change was needed. "I think it is nonsense to sell out to the Democrats on Capitol Hill," proclaimed Gingrich, who never forgave his fellow Republican. "For me to have voted for that compromise would have destroyed my effectiveness," the Minority Whip explained to justify his decision to oppose the president's budget compromise.

In 1994, under Gingrich's leadership, Republicans won control of Congress. The Georgian, and his style of partisanship, had delivered. As Speaker, Gingrich moved to finish the job that liberals had started in the 1970s by entrenching procedures that privileged centralized partisan power. Gingrich crushed any opportunity for committee chairs to act independently. The Speaker went further than the Democrats in the 1970s, appointing committee chairs directly from his office and relying on the Rules Committee—which he stacked with supporters—to craft the legislative schedule and adopt rules that would facilitate his goals. He handpicked loyalists such as Louisiana's Robert

 Livingston to chair Appropriations, Virginia's Thomas Bliley Jr. to chair the Energy and Commerce Committee, and Henry Hyde of Illinois to take over the Judiciary Committee, as well as several freshmen to seats on five major committees, including Ways and Means. The Speaker term-limited all committee chairs to six years. Republicans streamlined the committee referral process, granting his office full control over making the determination. According to the revised procedure, the Speaker would "designate a committee of primary jurisdiction upon the initial referral of a measure to a committee" and could send the measure to an additional referral.

Under Speaker Gingrich, ad hoc committees completed the takeover of agenda-setting from committee chairs. The normal rules of order were ignored in order to rush legislation through from start to finish. A product of the television age, Gingrich also commanded enormous media attention. For the first few months of his term, the Speaker convened daily news conferences to compete with President Clinton.

Gingrich, along with his counterpart in the Senate, Kansas senator Robert Dole, continued to rely on campaign money as another lever of influence. One of the first moves that Speaker Gingrich made was to appoint the chair of the RCCC. Of course, wielding the "mother's milk" of politics was not new. There was a long list of legislators, such as Lyndon Johnson, who figured out how controlling the purse strings of private donations would enhance their authority. But the scale and scope, as well as the sophistication, of these operations increased substantially over time. With congressional elections becoming increasingly nationalized, large organizations based in Washington had greater incentive to contribute to all races, not just the marquee matchups. In 1979, Congress had passed amendments to the Federal Election Campaign Act, which authorized unlimited donations to local and state party-building activities. These funds, which came to be known as "soft money," turned into a bonanza for party leaders. The lines between national, state, and local blurred. In 1980, the Republican National Committee raised and spent almost $9 million of "soft money." Democrats did the same in 1984, raising almost $27 million, which the national party earmarked for state registration and get-out-the-vote drives. Elizabeth Drew, a journalist whose beat was money and politics, warned that "in 1980 the national parties assumed the role of raising and distributing such funds—which was not the intent of the law—and have significantly expanded their use. Through an imaginative, and questionable, interpretation of the law, both parties now use soft money for Congressional as well as Presidential campaigns." Through soft money, the national party committees and congressional leadership PACs, barely relevant before, emerged as the giants in the room. They were fully staffed, operationally sophisticated, and computerized—a different world from the rudimentary system that had previously existed. Raising and spending campaign funds was no longer some kind of shady brown bag enterprise. With the cost of congressional campaigns continuing to skyrocket as a result of television, the ability of congressional leaders to help incumbents and challengers access funds was one of the most valuable tools they had.

As Speaker of the House, Gingrich didn't just centralize power but continued to ratchet up what maneuvers were deemed acceptable. In a dramatic confrontation with President Clinton in 1995–1996, Gingrich directed his caucus through two lengthy shutdowns of the federal government that would normalize that tactic in budget disputes. During the protracted standoff, the Speaker went so far as to threaten that House Republicans might not raise the federal debt ceiling, which would send the country into financial default. This came as a surprise to most political veterans. Congress had enacted the debt ceiling in 1917 as a way to provide more flexibility to the Treasury Department when it was running out of funds and to create an efficient process for fulfilling the nation's budgetary obligations. Whenever the budget required Treasury to take on additional debt, the House and Senate took a pro forma vote to raise the debt ceiling. The only other country to adopt a comparable mechanism was Denmark. Passage of the debt ceiling became routine. The only moment of crisis had taken place in 1979, when the Democratic Congress waited so long to pass the legislation (because they were haggling about how to stop a Republican drive for a balanced budget requirement) that the country technically slid into default. President Carter's Department of Treasury had immediately corrected the situation, however. In response to what happened, congressional Democrats didn't decide that this would be a new normal but, rather, the party took steps to make sure that it would never happen again. In 1979, the House adopted a proposal from Missouri representative Richard Gephardt, known as the "Gephardt Rule," that guaranteed that the federal debt ceiling would automatically increase whenever necessary. When the House agreed to the budget resolution, the rule stipulated that the clerk would provide a joint resolution that suspended the debt limit over the fiscal year of the budget resolution. Democratic majorities in both chambers worked with President Reagan to avert default in 1987 after a prolonged standoff over taxes and spending.

In the face-off with President Clinton in 1995, House Republicans were serious about going through with the threat. At the start of the session, the GOP suspended the Gephardt Rule, setting up the possibility of default. The House GOP was determined to obtain steep budgetary concessions from the president before agreeing to send him a bill. "I don't care what the price is," Gingrich warned. "I don't care if we have no executive offices and no bonds for sixty days—not this time." Gingrich's ultimatum made the threat far more serious than in the past. Rather than a lone member of the party announcing that he or she would symbolically cast a vote against raising the debt ceiling, knowing that the support to raise the ceiling was securely in place, this clash involved the Speaker of the House signaling what his entire caucus was prepared to do. Insisting on across-the-board spending cuts, Gingrich vowed that if Clinton didn't agree to their demands, Republicans would let the nation suffer the dire economic consequences and wait to "see how long they will last," referring to the president's fortitude. In the end, however, it was Gingrich who pulled back. In a game of chicken, the Republicans blinked first and sent the president a clean bill. Nonetheless, the elevation of the threat as a full-blown party strategy and the legitimization of two lengthy shutdowns were victories for Republicans who insisted that their party had to take the gloves off.

A couple of years later, Gingrich led the House Republicans in a different kind of hyperpartisan battle as the House voted to impeach President Clinton for having perjured himself about a sexual relationship with a White House intern named Monica Lewinsky and for having obstructed justice to stifle an investigation by Independent Prosecutor Kenneth Starr. Polls showed that large majorities of Americans didn't think Clinton's infraction was worthy of his being removed from office. Instead, they sensed that the impeachment was being driven by raw partisan objectives. Ironically, shortly before the Lewinsky scandal broke in January 1998, Speaker Gingrich had been secretly negotiating with Clinton over a bipartisan deficit-reduction package that would cut entitlement programs. The lure of partisanship, however, proved to be much stronger than the desire for a bipartisan policy breakthrough. Following a poor showing by Republicans in the 1998 midterms, and as a result of his own extramarital affair, the GOP pressured Gingrich into stepping down in 1999—the second Speaker to fall in about a decade; others would follow in the coming decades. Gingrich's successor, Congressman Dennis Hastert of Illinois, didn't change directions even though he maintained a lower profile in the media. Speaker Hastert continued to run his party, and the institution, with a strong hand. New Jersey Republican Christopher Smith, for instance, lost the chairmanship of the Veterans Affairs Committee for having allied with Democrats to secure additional funds for veterans. Under the "Hastert Rule," the Speaker, who after retiring would be sent to federal prison for making illegal bank withdrawals to pay off a former high school student of his whom he had sexually molested, would never bring a bill to vote unless it had the support of more than half of the majority party. Hastert allowed the use of congressional earmarks granted to increase from 2,838 in 1999 to 13,997 in 2005 as a way to reward and punish party members. In November 2004, he pushed through a rules change just to protect Majority Leader Tom DeLay, known as "the Hammer," if he was indicted on felony charges when he was being investigated for his role in Texas's questionable redistricting process one year earlier. DeLay was an even fiercer partisan tactician than his boss, refining a revolving door that he created between GOP staffers and the lobbyists on K Street, as well as brazen redistricting plans orchestrated by the national party, to make sure that no Republicans betrayed the congressional caucus. As DeLay said when retiring as a result of his scandals, "I found that it is customary in speeches such as these to reminisce about the good old days of political harmony and across-the-aisle camaraderie, and to lament the bitter, divisive partisan rancor that supposedly now weakens our—our democracy. Well, I can't do that because partisanship, Mr. Speaker, properly understood, is not a symptom of democracy's weakness but of its health and its strength, especially from the perspective of a political conservative."

The asymmetry was likewise evident in views of presidential power. Although both parties proved tolerant and supportive of a strong executive branch, Republicans advocated a vision of a commander in chief who was far less shackled by rules or norms than anything most Democrats imagined. As William Howell and Terry Moe argue, "Because most of the administrative state is the embodiment of progressive values, Presidents from the two parties respond to it very differently. Democratic Presidents support it, so they tend to approach presidential power in ways compatible with the administrative state's well-being, the laws that authorize and define it, and the continued pursuit of its many governmental missions. Republican Presidents staunchly oppose it, looking upon it not just with skepticism but with outright contempt. And as their party has grown more conservative, they have laid claim to increasingly extreme powers intended not only to control but also to retrench and sabotage significant portions of the federal bureaucracy."

Congressional Democrats likewise continued their drift to the left ideologically and were increasingly aggressive in their partisan tactics. Speaker Nancy Pelosi, whose term started in 2007, clamped down on internal dissent and made sure that committee chairs followed her directives rather than vice versa. Everyone knew that there would be hell to pay for crossing her. Senate Majority Leader Harry Reid (2007–2015), a former amateur boxer from Nevada, flexed his muscle by manipulating campaign money to push back against the growing individualism of the upper chamber. He stacked committees with people whom he could count on. When the Senate was crafting the details of President Barack Obama's Affordable Care Act in 2009 and 2010, Reid grew increasingly frustrated with committee leaders who were determined to find Republican votes for the bill, and pushed them to prioritize finding party-line support. Fed up with Republican obstruction of President Obama's nominations, in 2013 the Majority Leader invoked the "nuclear option" by ending the right to filibuster federal court and executive nominees (with the exception of the Supreme Court).

But Democratic polarization adhered to self-imposed limits that no longer existed with the GOP. As a party with a more diverse, big-tent electoral base, Democrats continued to include a sizable presence of moderates in both chambers; the House and Senate leadership privileged those voices. President Clinton promoted centrism from the White House, especially after the Republican takeover of Congress, going so far as to proclaim in 1996 that the "era of big government is over."

Congressional Democratic leaders also remained more wedded to traditional norms of governance and boundaries to partisan warfare. At some level, they had to. Democrats didn't keep themselves shackled out of the goodness of their hearts. To politicians who were committed to the role of the federal government, the ability of leaders to govern was essential, as was the functionality of Congress. Most in the Party of FDR and LBJ understood that gridlock disproportionately benefited their market-focused opponents who aimed to tie up the machinery of government.

The asymmetry in partisanship was bolstered by campaign finance. As single-issue organizations and individuals assumed a larger role as the source of campaign donations, legislators found themselves under growing pressure from forces that came from the extreme sides of the political spectrum. In general, the sources of Republican donations were much further to the right than Democratic contributors were to the left. Conservative donors were so ideologically driven that they preferred to avoid the party, perceiving it to be too moderate even after the rise of Gingrich, whereas liberal donors didn't see the need to make these distinctions.

While voters watched hyperpolarization fuel divisions over almost every issue, Democrats joined Republicans in keeping certain economic matters off the table altogether. With regard to market regulation and corporate power, a substantial number of Democrats felt that President Reagan and his successors in Congress had successfully pushed national debate to the right. In order to succeed, Democratic leaders perceived the need to be sensitive to the new tenor of the national discourse. Democrats were also being responsive to the fact that powerful businesses had mobilized in the 1970s to combat the expansion of policies that aimed to protect consumers, minorities, and the environment. Chief executives hedged their bets by spreading money all around and trying to make sure that at some level Democrats and Republicans would veer away from strong regulations and high tax policies. The choice was not only pragmatic. There was a strong current within Democratic thought in those years that genuinely believed market-based solutions to perennial policy problems, like poverty, could work. The donors were likewise encountering a growing number of prominent Democrats, all of whom had watched President Clinton rebound politically after Republicans won control of Congress in 1994, double down on the economic center despite frustration from progressives.

The effects were doubly corrosive. Voters were left with an unpalatable choice between two parties that were profoundly at odds on most questions while ignoring one of the most pertinent of all—an unequal economy that skewed toward the upper-income brackets. Frustrated working- and middle-class Americans felt that they had nowhere to turn.

Having one party that would be willing to go as far as the Republicans was not something that reformers imagined in the 1970s. For they had worked in a political environment where Democratic and Republican leaders generally respected the traditional trifecta of responsibilities. When deliberating over "responsible partisanship" in the 1970s, reformers had been thinking primarily in terms of parties that were responsible to the voters who elected them as well as rank-and-file members who were responsible for following through on their promises.

Considering the parties as being like two opposing teams of athletes on the playing field, reformers had assumed that there would be rules guiding the game, referees who would be able to enforce the rules, and an agreement among the competitors that everyone would abide by the rules. The kind of responsibility to which they had not devoted as much thought, the type that grew in importance after Gingrich and his generation rolled into town, was the need for officeholders to abide by functional norms and to respect guardrails. Less comparable to football or baseball, congressional politics was becoming more like professional wrestling where the "heel" sneaked "foreign objects" into the ring and threw the referee over the ropes so that anything could go. It was no surprise that the no-holds-barred Lee Atwater, one of the most influential consultants of the period, saw professional wrestling as a model for politics. Once the GOP embraced this basic political worldview, anything became possible.

The Gingrich generation of Republicans only became more powerful over time. Not only did their numbers increase within the House of Representatives, but several of them moved on to the Senate, such as Pennsylvania's Rick Santorum and Kansas's Sam Brownback, where they brought their slash-and-burn tactics to the upper chamber, elevating aggressive partisanship over the deliberative norms on which the Senate had prided itself. The political scientist Sean Theriault perceptively labeled them "The Gingrich Senators." As Wyoming Republican Alan Simpson acknowledged, "The rancor, the dissension, the disgusting harsh level came from those House members who came to the Senate. They brought it with 'em."

Unstable Majorities

If the GOP had moved in the direction they did, with Democrats retaining firm control of Congress, then the overall impact on polarization might have been less severe. But the electoral success of the modern Republican Party produced an era of unstable and insecure congressional majorities. The fact that neither Democrats nor Republicans could maintain tight control of the House and Senate ramped up the pressure on both parties to remain disciplined and intensify their tactics.

One turning point occurred in 1980, when Republicans gained control of the Senate. Democrats won a majority in the upper chamber in 1986, but eight years later the GOP ended virtually six decades of Democratic rule on Capitol Hill (with the exception of 1947–1949 and 1953–1955), winning both the House and Senate. Their dramatic victories did not produce the same kind of stable, long-term majorities that Democrats had enjoyed between the 1930s and the 1990s. As a result, congressional power turned into a seesaw. Democrats won back the Senate in 2001, both chambers in 2006, and the House in 2018. Republicans returned to power in the House in 2010 and in the Senate in 2014.

At the same time that congressional power frequently switched hands, the size of congressional majorities steadily shrank. In contrast to the 1960s, when Democrats claimed 66 percent of the Senate and 68 percent of the House in the eighty-ninth Congress, partisan divisions were nearly even in most of the twenty-first century, at times leaving the vice president to act as the tiebreaking vote in the Senate.

In the era of unstable majorities, the internal incentives for the parties to cooperate diminished. The political logic that flowed out of the state of one-party rule—which had pushed Democrats to accept some Republican proposals without fearing substantial electoral losses and Republicans to enter into negotiation with the Democrats if they wanted to remain relevant—was replaced by impulses that encouraged them to take unyielding partisan stands. As political scientist Frances Lee argued, legislators found themselves in a contentious environment where the rational path of decision-making was to distance themselves from, and to tear down, opponents. As Lee found, "Neither party . . . has suffered from the defeatism that characterized Republicans for so much of the preceding post–New Deal era." Because majorities were so minuscule, moreover, neither side in the House or Senate believed that they could afford to lose even one single vote or give an inch to their opponents as it might help them politically. Cooperation could come at the cost of majority power. For this reason, party leaders used every carrot and stick at their disposal to keep members in line. The rank and file did not always have to be forced into doing anything as they understood how any defection could detrimentally affect their party. The potential cost of taking an independent stand was a serious primary challenge backed by national party leaders and their formidable campaign war chests.

The opposition party, Lee showed, became more interested in "messaging," rhetoric that emphasized difference and not reconciliation. Messaging was about not just using certain types of words but also making heavy investments in advertising and public communications consultants.

In addition to prioritizing messaging over legislating, the party caucuses were selecting confrontational leaders over those who desired to break bread with opponents. In the case of the GOP, Lee documented that nine of the leadership contests in the Republican House Caucus between 1980 and 1988 went to the person whose reputation revolved around bipartisan negotiation, such as Robert Michel; after 1988, the GOP chose confrontation, such as Gingrich, in six of the nine contests that were held in the next four years.

The more competitive the House and Senate became, the nastier politicians acted toward one another. The stakes of every speech, every decision, and every vote felt immense. No matter how trivial the issue that was being debated, there was always a way to discern the imperative to stand one's ground. The competitive climate fueled a partisan arms race, with one side prepared to do almost anything.

Besides the fate of congressional power, legislators were acutely sensitive to the ways that their decisions about whether to be loyal to the party could affect presidential elections whose outcome was increasingly being determined by a handful of swing states and, within those states, narrow slivers of the population. As states rigidified in their partisan preferences, the kind of landslide victories that Presidents Johnson (1964), Nixon (1972), and Reagan (1984) had enjoyed were no longer likely. In late 2000, pollster Matthew Dowd wrote to one of George W. Bush's top advisors that the number of genuine swing voters was so small, there was little incentive to court them. Most self-described independents voted regularly for one party or the other, despite what they told pollsters. Electoral College margins that had frequently reached more than 70 percent (FDR won with 98.5 percent in 1936; Eisenhower with 86 percent in 1956; LBJ with 90.3 percent in 1964; and Reagan with 97.6 percent in 1984) disappeared, declining to 50.4 and 53.2 percent for

President George W. Bush in 2000 and 2004, respectively; 67.8 and 61.7 percent for President Barack Obama, in 2008 and 2012; 56.9 percent for President Donald Trump in 2016; and 56.8 percent for President Joe Biden in 2020. Under these conditions, the marginal impact from handing the other party any kind of victory, no matter how narrow, could be to anger valuable pockets of Americans who would be critical to delivering the votes needed to reach 270 Electoral College votes. In contrast to FDR, presidents have become increasingly partisan. They counted on and coordinated with the congressional wing of the party, considered partisan factors in making their decisions, and in some cases—with Republicans doing more work than Democratic presidents until Bill Clinton—raised and directed resources to party building.

The more legislators engaged in aggressive behavior, the deeper the wounds from the partisan wars. Just as in a prolonged military battle, the experience of serving in public office generated bitter feelings of recrimination among representatives and senators who, or whose predecessors, had been in the trenches. Each generation of legislators entered office determined to get retribution for what had happened in the past to their colleagues or themselves.

It was an unending, vicious cycle. It wasn't a surprise that Democrats felt vindicated when Speaker Gingrich was fined for ethics violations of his own in 1997 and then forced to resign from power one year later. It was hard for Democrats to not feel downright joyful, with memories of Wright's resignation speech on their minds, as Gingrich explained his decision by saying, "I'm willing to lead but I'm not willing to preside over people who are cannibals." Insisting that he didn't want to gloat, former Speaker Wright compared Gingrich to "an arsonist who sets fire to his own building without stopping to realize the flames are going to consume his own apartment."

The centrifugal forces at work in Congress were fueled and magnified by the institutions that surrounded it. The aftermath of Vietnam and Watergate generated more sources of division, not fewer. The media underwent dramatic transformation during those decades. The rise of cable television, the growth of conservative talk radio, and the advent of the internet created a media ecosystem that favored legislators who played to sensation and discord. The decisions by the Federal Communications Commission in 1987 to end the Fairness Doctrine meant that radio and television shows could produce partisan broadcasts without any fear of legal trouble. As local newspapers and television shows were shuttered, legislators who craved press attention had no option other than to find space on the usually toxic and divisive national media platforms where fierce argument was rewarded and sober conversation shunned. Despite the best efforts to regulate campaign finance after Watergate, the private money that fueled partisan division also continued to find ways around the law. After Congress closed the door to soft money with the McCain-Feingold reforms in 2002, single-issue organizations, wealthy issue-oriented donors, and shadowy tax-exempt organizations (527s and 501(c)(4)s) were able to funnel huge amounts of money into the coffers of politicians who stuck to the party line. In 2010, the Supreme Court's Citizens United decision opened the floodgates to unlimited donations. In 2012, outside groups spent approximately \$27 million on Senate primary election ads, compared to \$3 million in 2004. They spent \$20 million on House primaries, in contrast to $2 million eight years earlier. Political party committees tried to coordinate their efforts with these groups. These organizations tended to be even more extreme than the parties themselves, unfettered by the need to preserve coalitions, and able to funnel money without being bound by significant limitations or accountability requirements. The changes have moved "money from accountable actors, the political parties, to unaccountable groups," noted law professor Nathan Persily. He added, "The parties are accountable not only because of more stringent contribution disclosure requirements but also by their role in actual governance with their ties to congressional and executive branch officials and their involvement with legislative decision-making." With confirmations, for instance, dark money flowed to senators who would support or oppose the nominees that best served the interest of Republicans or Democrats. And increasingly sophisticated redistricting techniques perfected the art of creating solidly red or blue lines, which, at the marginal level, pushed House representatives to the extreme edges of the political spectrum. Although a good deal of this money did not go through party committees, the single issues that donors focused on aligned neatly with party platforms. Even popular culture played into the tensions by producing more movies, television shows, and books sliced and diced in order to fit into commercially lucrative siloed worldviews. President George W. Bush's admirers could flock to watch *24*, a major network show on television about a counterterrorist agent named Jack Bauer (played by Kiefer Sutherland), who did whatever was necessary, including torture, to stop national security threats. They tuned into Darryl Worley's "Have You Forgotten?" for his blistering words about antiwar protesters.

Liberal Americans watched *The West Wing* and listened to the Dixie Chicks (now the Chicks) who were blacklisted for being critical of the administration and the war.

Going Off the Rails from the Tea Party to Trump

The Tea Party Republicans who came to town after the 2010 midterms were even more extreme. The younger Republicans who came of age watching the normalization of Gingrich's style of partisanship had no qualms. But as often occurs with political revolution, the new generation thought their predecessors had not gone far enough. They were also frustrated with and disillusioned by Republican president George W. Bush, whom they derided as a "big government conservative" who had grown far too comfortable with Washington. "What use is a Republican to us, if all they do is vote with Democrats?" asked an early Tea Party activist, Christina Botteri.

They hated President Barack Obama, for reasons ranging from his race to his policy agenda, and felt that the GOP needed to do whatever was necessary to stop him. The new generation of Republicans was fully prepared to refuse to raise the debt ceiling in 2011, if necessary, in an effort to extract draconian budget concessions from President Obama. Like Gingrich in 1995, the GOP suspended the Gephardt Rule, which had been reinstated. Following stern warnings from the president that he would not negotiate with hostage-takers, that was exactly what the administration ended up doing. The result was hundreds of billions in federal spending cuts in exchange for preventing the United States from going into default.

Obama had no other choice. With the GOP controlling the House and sending strong signals of being willing to pull this nuclear trigger, the president felt that he was backed into a corner. His lawyers dissuaded him from invoking the Fourteenth Amendment, which included a provision that stipulated that the "validity of the public debt of the United States . . . shall not be questioned." Although the conflict was resolved, the risks had been so grave that Standard and Poor's announced it would downgrade the credit rating for the United States. "The political brinksmanship of recent months," they stated in the press release, "highlights what we see as America's governance and policymaking becoming less stable, less effective, and less predictable than what we previously believed." "I think some of our members may have thought the default issue was a hostage you might take a chance at shooting," Senator Mitch McConnell, who helped rein in his House colleagues, commented. "Most of us didn't think that. What we did learn is this—it's a hostage that's worth ransoming." While in 2013, President Obama stood the GOP down when they tried to use the debt-ceiling strategy, the precedent was set; the bar had been lowered. Another process had been weaponized.

Tea Party Republicans also deployed explosive rhetoric that made Gingrich seem tame. Emulating the former Speaker's mantra of saying anything in pursuit of victory, they said anything. They found a powerful platform on Fox News television and conservative talk radio, as well as the expanding universe of social media, where, without any pushback, they could characterize Democrats as left-wing socialists intent on destroying America. They abandoned any concern about mutual respect, instead rejecting the legitimacy of the opposition. Most famously, a number of Republicans joined or tolerated the Birther movement in 2011, going on the airwaves and online to question the birthplace—and thus the legitimacy—of the nation's first Black American president. Others in the GOP who didn't join the crusade stood aside quietly as their counterparts did.

Tea Party Republicans went so far as to render their own leadership less secure. Drawing inspiration from Newt Gingrich, who had risen to power by toppling the Democratic Speaker Jim Wright in 1989—and then who was himself brought down by fellow Republicans almost ten years later—they wanted to demonstrate that even their own Speakers could not afford to ignore the concerns of average members. Unlike the 1970s, when congressional reforms aimed to achieve a balance between strong Speakers and a strong rank and file, the Tea Party leaned heavily toward the bottom-up. Just as they used the debt ceiling as a bludgeon against Democrats, Republicans weaponized House Rule IX to ensure that their Speakers had less wiggle room to defy angry factions within the caucus. The rule established in the nineteenth century empowered a single representative to introduce a privileged "motion to vacate" the office of the Speaker and required that the Speaker put up the resolution for a vote within two legislative days. At that point, a majority of the House could vote to render the Speakership vacant. Realizing that the rule had the potential to produce damaging instability if normalized, the motion to vacate had remained largely dormant for much of congressional history. The biggest exception had occurred in 1910 when Democrat Albert Burleson introduced a motion to vacate Speaker Cannon (the motion failed though reforms stripped the Speakership of many powers). Though House Republicans drafted a resolution in 1997 to threaten Speaker Gingrich, he resigned before it was introduced.

The potential for the caucus to vacate the office of the Speaker became much more real in 2015 when North Carolina Tea Party Republican Mark Meadows filed a motion against John Boehner (R-OH). Though Meadows's resolution never came up for a vote, it was a big part of the reason that Boehner resigned from the Speakership in 2015. "My first job as speaker," Boehner said, "is to protect the institution. It had become clear to me that this prolonged leadership turmoil would do irreparable harm to the institution." Boehner later admitted that he had been dealing with "legislative terrorists." Sensing that fellow Republicans were still willing to deploy the motion to vacate after they rejected his demand to reform the rule, which he labeled a "weapon," Paul Ryan's (R-WI) tenure as Speaker left him beholden to the Tea Party. Seeking to reestablish order in 2019, House Democrats under Speaker Nancy Pelosi pushed through a change to Rule IX that required a motion to vacate the office of the Speaker obtain the support of a majority of one party.

Senator McConnell practiced an equally intense style of partisanship, but in a more silent style. The senator was less interested in rhetorical bombast than in roughhouse procedural warfare. While avoiding the glare of television as much as possible, McConnell privileged partisan power with equal verve. "You are only as good as the next election," he liked to say. As the leader of the GOP, he demonstrated a willingness to bend or break traditional norms and procedure to advantage his party. Filibusters were in his bloodstream and he was prepared to stand in the way of every presidential appointment that came his way. The senator embraced the polarization of the judicial nomination and confirmation process. Under his leadership, there were fewer committee hearings or courtesy meetings for nominees. From the first day of the Obama administration he set out to obstruct, with the intention of making Obama a one-term president. Given that voters tend to blame presidents for results, McConnell calculated that the legislative obstruction would not harm the GOP politically as much as it would the president who would appear to be ineffective. One of McConnell's top allies, Senator Robert Bennett, recalled, "Mitch said, 'We have a new president with an approval rating in the seventy percent area. We do not take him on frontally. We find issues where we can win, and we begin to take him down, one issue at a time. We create an inventory of losses, so it's Obama lost on this, Obama lost on that. And we wait for the time where the image has been damaged to the point where we can take him on.'" The most dramatic moment occurred in 2016, when McConnell refused to hold a vote, or convene office meetings, after President Obama nominated judge Merrick Garland, a cautious and moderate legal mind with broad bipartisan support, to replace Supreme Court Justice Antonin Scalia. McConnell made up a precedent to legitimate his decision. Because of his efforts, the seat remained open until a Republican was in the White House in 2017, part of McConnell's ongoing efforts to fill the federal courts with conservative nominees drawn from the lists of the Federalist Society.

With the GOP and Fox News now working as a well-oiled machine, the loosely organized Tea Party got from Fox News what it didn't previously have, including a united group of followers and an entire media infrastructure to go along with it. For conservative media stars such as Andrew Breitbart, the access that the new partisan media offered the right was a way to level the playing field with liberals. "The Democrats have the Big Three Networks and major news dailies as their offensive line, and a starting backfield of Hollywood celebrities and academia," Breitbart argued. "Fortunately, however, the New Media comes with rules that level the playing field. The virtual newsroom at my Big websites... is an exercise in no-huddle offense, where citizens can call audibles and get in the game. And it has forced the Democrat-Media Complex to finally play some defense." The conservative media ecosystem dominated red America. In 2014, a study by Pew found that, among conservatives, 47 percent considered Fox News to be their primary source for information about politics. Of the conservatives surveyed, 88 percent trusted Fox News and most received feeds from Facebook that were consistent with their own views. Liberals consumed their news from a much broader number of outlets and they were "less unified in their media loyalty." Conspiratorial rumors gained much more traction in right-wing information streams. The maturation of the internet would vastly expand the platforms available, and with few editorial or production controls, disseminating partisan information or disinformation became much easier. Legislators (and their staff) became a presence on social media sites, tweeting and posting to get out their messages and go after their opponents. Although the ability of information silos to shape public opinion remains up for debate, the information gateways certainly solidified worldviews.

As one party played by rules and the other didn't, the result was a massive imbalance that made political warfare much more unpredictable and destabilizing. Democrats found themselves at a distinct disadvantage because of their unwillingness to go all the way. As singer-songwriter Jason Isbell stated, "Well, you know, if you're the dirtiest fighter in a fight, you're gonna win. You bite somebody's ear off, you're probably gonna beat 'em. And if there are no rules—or if the rules keep changing according to whoever won the last fight—you're fucked. Because all of a sudden they're like, 'Hey, this guy's a really good ear biter. *Let's make it where you can bite ears!*'"

The hyperpolarization of American politics reached new levels with the presidency of Donald Trump between 2017 and 2021. The former real estate mogul and reality television star acted like a human wrecking ball. Although there were many distinct elements about him and his style, he was a product of the age and had an instinctive grasp of how polarization defined public life. Rather than running away from this reality, he embraced it. President Trump violated every norm with reckless abandon, going so far as to use foreign aid to Ukraine, which was under serious threat from Russia, as a chit to obtain political dirt on former vice president Joe Biden and calling North Korean president Kim Jong Un "rocket man" during a speech at the United Nations. Trump and the congressional GOP worked closely together. The president enjoyed a 98.7 percent success rate in 2017 in securing the Republican support that he needed for bills. The number fell slightly in his second year but, overall, remained high. The partisanship of the GOP was so totalizing that the leadership protected the president during two historic impeachments, including the one that revolved around Trump's role in an insurrection. Senator McConnell publicly condemned Trump on the floor of his chamber, blaming him for being "practically and morally responsible" for the violence that unfolded on January 6, but only after making sure the Senate voted against the articles of impeachment. Soon after making his statement, McConnell acknowledged to a reporter that he would support Trump in 2024 if Trump was the nominee.

Partisan incentives were becoming so strong that even the sense of shame started to fade within the party. President Trump used his historic impeachments as a basis to rally supporters, solidify his standing in the GOP, and define his strengths. Never did he express any sense of remorse or apology. In doing so, Trump rendered one of the main features of impeachment—the ability of Congress to wield the process as a threat to scare presidents into better behavior—virtually meaningless. At the same time that "impeachment talk" has become normalized, the solidification of a party stance within the Republican Caucus that was seemingly immune from the threat severely undercut the efficacy of the constitutional mechanism. Meanwhile, there has been a similar phenomenon on Capitol Hill, where being censured has become a badge of honor and a fundraising opportunity for Republicans rather than a source of ignominy. Each revelation of wrongdoing, scandal, or indictment has been greeted with email and text blasts to supporters asking for increased financial support. After defiantly posting his mug shot on Twitter, following a fourth indictment since his presidency ended, Trump raised $7.1 million in a twenty-four-hour period. His reelection team didn't run away from the news but rather sold merchandise, from posters to T-shirts to bumper stickers, featuring the photograph.

At the same time that Trump depended and capitalized on partisanship, he made political parties one of his many targets. As he has done with almost every institution, Trump railed against parties, using rhetoric that helped to further delegitimize them. Democrats were simply a partisan organization out to destroy him; the Republicans were led by an establishment that could not be trusted, either. Although Trump's term came to an end, the arguments he made lived on. He helped ensure that as institutions the parties would be even more hated, distrusted, and ignored.

By January 2021, when Joe Biden started his presidency, political scientists John Sides, Chris Tausanovitch, and Lynn Vavreck found that most of the electorate had "calcified." It was nearly impossible to flip significant blocks of voters anymore. Persuasion was less relevant than mobilization. Without big electoral swings, parties hammered away at each other on the smallest of issues. Just as in Congress, this intensified the rationale for the parties to refuse to give any ground.

The polling about political division has only moved in one direction: from bad to worse, assuming one believes that hyperpartisan division is harmful. According to the most recent data, *New York Times* writer Thomas Edsall reported, the subjects that caused Americans to divide along party lines keep widening. Democrats and Republicans perceive unbridgeable differences over worldviews and understandings of nationalism, not just policies and issues. As political scientist Marc Hetherington explained to Edsall: "Because political beliefs now reflect deeply held worldviews about how the world ought to be—challenging traditional ways of doing things on the one hand and putting a brake on that change on the other—partisans look across the aisle at each other and absolutely do not understand how their opponents can possibly understand the world as they do." Psychologists at the University of Limerick found that American voters have become much sharper and more sensitive about discerning small clues that inform them whether a total stranger is a Republican or Democrat. Affective partisanship, as Lilliana Mason has argued, is rooted in feeling and emotion, making political attachment much more intense.

With Democrats and Republicans in perpetual competition for control of Congress, and the GOP adopting an anything-goes mindset, the promise of partisanship in the 1970s has turned into the source of the nation's worst nightmares. With almost every major public institution fostering division, the partisanship that reformers had championed became something very different from what they originally had in mind, a form of political combat so toxic and destructive that it brought the nation to a dangerous place where it was actually necessary for the president of the United States to make a televised speech on the eve of the 2022 midterm elections to say: "What we're doing now is going to determine whether democracy will long endure. It, in my view, is the biggest of questions: whether the American system that prizes the individual, bends toward justice, and depends—depends on the rule of law—whether that system will prevail. This is the struggle we're now in: a struggle for democracy, a struggle for decency and dignity, a struggle for prosperity and progress, a struggle for the very soul of America itself."

One of Trump's most consequential short-term legacies on Capitol Hill was to inspire a new generation of MAGA Republicans to enter into elected office who were even more extreme than the Tea Party. When it came to the Speakership, the rambunctious Republican foot soldiers of the House were not intimidated by their own generals. As a sign of how far they were willing to go, in 2023, in exchange for throwing their support behind California Republican Kevin McCarthy as Speaker of the House, MAGA Republicans pressured him into dismantling Pelosi's reform by once again making it possible for just one member to introduce a motion to vacate the office of the Speaker. When McCarthy subsequently decided to cooperate with Democrats to fund the government, Florida Republican Matt Gaetz deployed Rule IX and removed McCarthy from the office. With narrow margins and a rambunctious caucus, McCarthy's Speakership lasted only 269 days, making it the third shortest Speakership in American history (Speaker Michael Kerr died in the middle of his term in 1876 and Theodore Pomery was elected on the final day of the 40th Congress in 1869). House Republicans, after multiple rounds of voting that lasted for three weeks, finally replaced McCarthy with Louisiana Republican Mike Johnson, a legislator who was to the right of the right. Yet Speaker Johnson likewise found himself under the same threat. Georgia representative Marjorie Taylor Greene—who said she didn't care if the Speakership turned into a "revolving door"—sounded the alarm by announcing that she intended to push for a vote to depose Johnson if he allied with Democrats to keep the government open and pass critical legislation with aid for Ukraine, Israel, and Taiwan. "Being the Speaker of the House nowadays is like being Leonardo DiCaprio's girlfriend—you hang on as long as you can," joked late-night television host Jimmy Kimmel. Without any sense of irony, even the founding father of smashmouth partisanship, Newt Gingrich, admitted that the party had gone too far: "The demons ... unleashed by going after [Kevin] McCarthy are still out there. You can't govern by shooting yourself in the head every day." Speaker Johnson called Greene's bluff, deciding that the bill was more important than his job. Enough Republicans sided with him temporarily to secure his position when he worked through a bipartisan coalition to reach his objective. Most important in shaping their decision was that many in the House GOP were sensitive to how the perception of chaos among voters could greatly harm the party's prospects of retaining their slim majority in the 2024 elections. Trump weighed in to throw his support behind Johnson.

Without reforming the rules or changing the internal party culture, however, the foundation of the Speakership will remain shaky. The fragility of leadership had layered yet another governing challenge on top of the rest. Hyperpartisanship without leaders who can act with some autonomy is a recipe for intensified dysfunction.

Toward Responsible Partisanship Circa the 2020s

Hyperpartisanship is destructive. Few observers are eager to defend the status quo. The trauma of the past few years, particularly January 6, has left few Americans satisfied with the way our politics works.

But the major alternatives each pose significant problems of their own. *Madisonians* ignore the real need for big government interventions, downplaying the dysfunctional elements of our constitutional design. *Nonpartisanship* imagines a fictitious political world where deep electoral divisions magically disappear and an expert-driven governing structure can design policies that command broad interest and support. Based on American history since the Civil War, *third-partyism* doesn't have much of a chance of unseating either of the two deeply entrenched parties. The depth of Democratic and Republican strength, combined with the state-by-state challenges posed by the Electoral College, means that third parties are more likely to help elect one of the two mainstream candidates. *Bipartisanship* has challenges of its own, as the nation learned in the decades between the 1920s and the 1970s, which included its tendency to privilege cabals of leaders operating without transparency. Moreover, given how divided Americans are on core issues, the possibility of bipartisanship would be difficult to achieve as the norm. *Presidentialism* ignores the long history of abusing power that has resulted from executive-centered government.

The best and most realistic alternative to hyperpartisanship is *responsible partisanship*. But what Washington needs is an understanding of responsible partisanship that differs significantly from what was envisioned in APSA's 1950 report, when political scientists were concerned primarily about party leaders who were responsible to their rank and file and rank-and-file members who were responsible to the party platform. In the 2020s, responsible partisanship must revolve around strong parties that adhere to guardrails and compete within clear parameters, ensuring some degree of stability and functional governance despite our divisions.

With responsible partisanship, elected officials would once again respect and balance the trifecta of responsibilities that a healthy democracy requires besides attention to the needs of constituents within the district or state: partisanship, governance, and the protection of institutions.

An era of responsible partisanship would empower leaders to make tough decisions while being checked from abusing power, it would offer greater coherence to political competition and negotiation, it would provide a means for continuing to centralize deliberations while allowing all members pathways to participation, it would create a means for the electorate to express core differences of opinion within the mainstream political process, and it would provide mechanisms to hold leaders accountable for their actions. When one party has unified control of the White House and Congress, responsible partisanship expands the range of opportunities to pass bold legislation tackling big problems ordinarily left off the agenda. It is notable and relevant that even in our current era of hyperpartisan dysfunction, forceful party leadership has been integral to moving major legislation through Congress, as was evident with the role that Speaker Pelosi and Senate Majority Leader Reid played in the passage of the Affordable Care Act. Legislative entrepreneurs who specialize in particular issues have tended to do best when working with the leadership. To be sure, hyperpartisanship has vastly diminished the odds for major legislation when control of the government or Congress is divided. Yet even under these difficult circumstances, responsible partisanship can ensure voters have competing participants who defend principled positions and who have the standing within their respective caucuses to guide negotiations toward a compromise that is as effective, acceptable, and as lasting as possible. Party leaders, with their massive platform, are in a unique position to legitimate unpopular deals with their base.

The need for two distinct parties is substantial. Voters are deeply divided and they need choices within the political system to express their disagreement. The divisions span from the elite to mass level. Even scholars who in the 1990s questioned whether the cleavages within the electorate were as great as most people thought, today see through the prism of red and blue. Sociologist Alan Wolfe, who published a landmark book in the 1990s, *One Nation, After All,* recently acknowledged: "I don't know if [Trump's] a political genius or just instinctively knows something, but he sure has exacerbated the shocks, and I don't know how we are going to recover from him."

The hyperpartisanship of recent decades has not halted progress in all areas, as Congress still has shown the capacity to deal with defense spending, annual spending bills, and immediate crises. Biden made unexpected headway on several issues, including military assistance, infrastructure, green jobs, and anti-China policies. But hyperpartisanship has severely hampered the federal government, making it more difficult to address vital issues like climate change, immigration, gun control, public health, racial justice, and more. To be sure, many Republicans are satisfied with this status quo. It meshes with their rightward opposition to any government intervention whatsoever. If "government is the problem," as President Reagan famously quipped in his 1981 inaugural address, then the nation can live with gridlock. But others disagree. After all, the nation can't afford to have a federal government that can only take bold action under extraordinary conditions like a global pandemic. Government is as integral to American life as are private markets and individual rights. Indeed, these work hand in hand. Responsible partisanship, with capable legislators, will vastly improve the odds for Washington to be more responsive to national needs.

Just as in the Progressive Era and the 1970s, moving from one period of politics to another will require reforms to occur across different institutions and political sectors. More state governments will have to change their redistricting processes in order to grant authority to nonpartisan or bipartisan bodies. Doing so can result in a larger number of competitive House districts and thus diminish some of the pressure that representatives feel to toe the party line. Experiments in rank-order voting and proportional representation will help us to discern whether alternative electoral processes can generate countervailing pressure to the hyperpartisan imperative. Reforms to congressional primaries, such as switching to a single day primary for congressional nominees, have also been floated to try reducing the frequency of challenges from extremists who push incumbents toward hyperpartisan positions. Public investment in investigative journalism, innovative commercial initiatives, and local news outlets that provide high-quality, nonpartisan reporting will be necessary to break through our current crisis of rampant partisan news and disinformation. The presidential primary system must be reimagined once again so that a new process can work against the race to the bottom where candidates feel pressure to appeal to the most extreme activists in their party as well as feed reporters looking for explosive statements but who can provide the airtime needed to win. Constitutional amendments might be the only way to break free from the entrenched anti-majoritarian power of the Electoral College and the Senate.

But Capitol Hill must be the place to start the project of reform. The reasons are clear. Congress will always be at the center of the nation's democratic processes, so it is the best place to begin any process of transformation. "Undoubtedly, an experienced corps of experts can explore policy alternatives and select solutions to problems more expeditiously and more intelligently than a legislature," wrote political scientist Nelson Polsby, "but legislatures have learned to do this tolerably well and in addition can test alternatives against the demanding criterion of political acceptability in ways not readily available to experts." Legislators establish the tenor of political debate throughout Washington. The House and Senate retain immense constitutional authority, which enables the chambers to influence the dynamics of decision-making and political competition. And despite the distance between members of Congress and voters, the legislative branch remains the part of government that is most susceptible to democratic pressure.

So, what can be done within Congress to replace hyperpartisanship with responsible partisanship?

Disarming Weapons of Hyperpartisan Destruction

The process of reform should begin by removing some of the worst procedures that legislators have weaponized for partisan advantage. Eliminating or containing these tools is akin to arms control. Although bad actors will continue to find ways to engage in destructive behavior, seizing pivotal parts of the arsenal of mass partisan destruction can diminish the odds for the worst damage to be inflicted.

In recent years, no partisan weapon has been quite as destabilizing as the federal debt ceiling. The obligation for Congress to raise the debt ceiling has become artillery that Republicans have regularly and dangerously deployed in their budget battles, at least when a Democrat is in the White House. There have been several occasions since 1995 when the GOP marched the entire country toward the fiscal cliff. Although each crisis has generated discussions of how presidents can use their power to avert catastrophe, such as invoking the Fourteenth Amendment or minting an uber-coin, a better strategy would be to eliminate the provision altogether.

There has been growing interest in adopting a legislative fix. In 2022, Brookings Institution economist Louise Sheiner testified to the House Budget Committee that the debt ceiling served no purpose and never even achieved its goals: "Bickering over the debt ceiling is a waste of time and energy, creates unnecessary uncertainty, threatens the benefits of issuing the world's safest asset, and undermines public confidence in our political institutions." Willem Buiter, former chief economist at Citibank, argued that a better solution "would be to assign to Congress, through legislation, the 'deemed authority' to raise the debt ceiling automatically (assuming it is binding, as it is today) in every current and future period by the amount of the deficit implied by the Congressionally determined and Presidentially approved federal spending and tax programs." The problem has become so acute that even former treasury secretary Robert Rubin, hardly a radical, argued in frustration that "raising the debt limit, as lawmakers have finally done, is important but insufficient. Responsible lawmakers should aim to do something more ambitious, and with far more potential benefit to the American economy: eliminate the debt limit entirely."

Without reverting to the pre-1917 process of requiring legislators to take a vote each time the federal government required more funds, legislation could end the debt ceiling and grant the Department of the Treasury the authority it needs to issue new debt when the president requests it. Some believe the solution would come from permanently reinstating the Gephardt Rule. Another option, floated by Senator McConnell, would place the onus of increasing debt levels entirely on the shoulders of the president. McConnell's proposal would guarantee that presidents automatically obtain the debt levels necessary to pay for programs, and the political costs of having to request more money, unless Congress is able to muster veto-proof majorities to override him or her. The debt ceiling could also be raised through the reconciliation process, which can't be filibustered, and to levels that would prevent it from being broken in a foreseeable long time span.

The filibuster is the next partisan weapon that needs to be reformed or dismantled. Since the mid-1970s, the filibuster has been used to bring the legislative process to a grinding halt on both important and trivial issues. The filibuster has produced the worst of all possible worlds. The parties dig into intense combat at the same time that the odds of passing major legislation diminish, given that majority control of the House and Senate is not enough for the president's party to enact bills. Perpetual filibusters impose a bar so high for passing bills in the upper chamber that it dissuades elected officials from even trying to tackle many crucial problems. "The filibuster," said Adam Jentleson, who worked as deputy chief of staff for Senate Majority Leader Reid, "is a tool to preserve the status quo and make it harder to change." Why would a rational Senate majority, and the president with whom they are allied, invest political capital to pursue comprehensive immigration reform knowing they will require a bloc of votes from an opposition party that will never deliver coalitional support? The answer is they usually don't. The easier and more understandable path has been to move on.

The filibuster intensifies dysfunctional hyperpartisanship, not deliberation. By enshrining anti-majoritarian requirements in the process, filibusters have allowed the Senate minority to act ruthlessly. The minority party can easily block non-budgetary proposals that have strong popular support. Knowing that a filibuster threat exists has often been sufficient to shut down debate before it even begins. The minority party—especially in an age of insecure majorities—has little reason to cooperate with the majority. Although there are times when the filibuster has moved the majority toward compromise, what is more striking are the issues that never receive serious consideration.

In those rare moments when parties have won unified control of the White House and Congress, a disciplined minority has been able to block legislation. As a result, the parties end up making grandiose promises to appeal to a polarized electorate, sometimes winning the power of the majority and creating the conditions that should produce strong party action, but nonetheless they understand that those ideas will never come to fruition. As journalist Ezra Klein argued, "Even if the voters' chosen party does win power, it can't enact the agenda it has promised, as it is almost impossible to win 60 Senate seats, and otherwise, the filibuster blocks most of what parties promise to do. As a result, rather than judging the results of the agenda they voted for, voters are left assessing why so little has happened, and trying to understand who is to blame for their problems going unsolved." Ending the filibuster or significantly lowering the number needed for cloture, and requiring senators to actually hold the floor when filibustering, would make Congress more responsive to majoritarian demands. Without a filibuster, the minority party would have less ability to bring Washington to a complete standstill.

Some of the air would be let out of the majority leadership as well, since filing for cloture would become less important. Strong parties could use the limited windows of opportunity to enact important changes. Like the majority, a minority without the perpetual threat of the supermajority filibuster would find greater incentive to cooperate if they don't want to be on the losing side of a debate.

Reconciliation, which has become the main "majoritarian exception," as political scientist Molly Reynolds has called it, is an inadequate solution. Reconciliation is a messy and irrational method for formulating policy that is ordinarily used only once or twice a year. Just occasionally has the process offered a successful path to legislative productivity. When it has been used, policies are squeezed into the byzantine budget process, designed in ways that aim to improve the odds that proposals receive a good "score" from the Congressional Budget Office (namely, that it won't add to the deficit) and will be able to survive the scrutiny of the Senate Parliamentarian, an unelected official who rules on what can and can't be included. The "Byrd Rule," named for former Senate Majority Leader Robert Byrd, requires that the only legitimate measures must be budget-related and can't increase the deficit beyond a ten-year period. Many policy problems are thus shunted aside. Gimmicks are used to squeeze as much as possible into this process. The goal of finding the best and most-effective policy design falls by the wayside.

Filibuster reform is possible. It has been done before. In 1972, Senate Majority Whip Byrd instituted a two-track system. In 1975, the number needed for cloture was lowered. In 2013, Senate Democrats ended filibusters for federal judicial and executive nominations, and the Republican Senate did the same for the Supreme Court in 2017.

Another disarmament reform that has been floated would deal with the Senate confirmation process, which has reached a near crisis point as major jobs remained unfilled by permanent officials under President Biden. To overcome some of the partisan obstruction that continues to stifle the pace of confirmations would require either to remove certain secondary positions from the process, turning them into non-confirmed appointments, or to establish executive commissions to fill these jobs. There have also been proposals to broaden the Senate's "privileged" nomination calendar by allowing a greater range of appointments to circumvent the committees.

Finally, campaign finance must be part of any serious reform agenda. There is an urgent need to curb the power of private money in congressional campaigns. Control over campaign funds has enabled party leaders, large individual donors, and single-issue interest groups and PACs to place legislators in a vise whereby moving away from extreme positions becomes professionally perilous. Members also have to spend more time raising money than ever before in the institution's history. The pressures on candidates to secure dollars are too all-consuming. Incumbents are expected to raise enough so that they can donate unused funds to the congressional campaign committees for challengers in other states and districts. Members are constantly scrambling for funds in what they refer to as "call time," which has taken up a longer amount of every working day. Under these difficult conditions, every representative and senator faces the strong temptation to appeal to extreme sources, whether from party PACs or independent single-issue donors, who will most easily dole out money to loyal supporters.

There are several steps that Congress can take that would partially or fully close the spigot on the flow of private money. The grandest option would be to create a system of public finance for congressional campaigns. Public funds would vastly reduce the need for elected officials to kowtow to lobbyists, donors, and single-issue interest groups. Diminishing private money in politics is inherently better for the health of democratic institutions while freeing up elected officials to spend more energy on the hard work of governance. If the sources of campaign funds were more reliable and didn't primarily emanate from interests who insist on elected officials sticking to the extreme ends of the spectrum, legislators could be more sober in evaluating the most urgent partisan moves.

There are other concrete incremental steps, albeit less bold, that could temper the excesses of the system. Short of a full public finance process would be a targeted public finance system that improves the quality of political parties as institutions connecting voters to elected officials. Reimposing the limitations that the Supreme Court dismantled in Citizens United (2010) would be a crucial measure. Seeking to reverse the decision, California Democrat Adam Schiff has proposed legislation recognizing that the Constitution did not limit the ability of Congress or the states to create reasonable restrictions on private contributions and independent spending. Regulations also need to be crafted in ways that incentivize expenditures on genuine local party-building rather than on high-cost campaign professionals disconnected from the electorate. Furthermore, Congress needs to tackle the problem of undisclosed spending by tax-exempt organizations, which has been one area where rules and enforcement have been weakest.

Reforms to expand incentives for small donations should also continue to be put into place. Efforts in some states and localities have attempted to encourage smaller contributions over large donations. Seattle introduced vouchers, financed through property taxes, that voters can use to make donations, while New York City has provided matching funds for contributions that are $175 or less. As Mark Schmitt of New America has argued, "Instead of trying to limit money, and failing—let's empower everyone. What if everyone could write a check, not necessarily a fat one, but enough that, together with others, it could make it possible for people to run who don't have access to the very wealthy or ensure that the concerns and preferences of ordinary voters carry at least some weight in the process." Though small donations from regular voters are beneficial to democracy, scholars have noted that those who donate tend to be among the most ideologically extreme.

This means that encouraging small donations must be coupled with reforms to strengthen the financial role of parties. The combination of small donations from the most ideologically extreme voters, dark money, and independent expenditures has offered candidates multiple avenues to obtain the campaign funds they need while circumventing the parties. Political scientists Raymond La Raja and Brian Schaffner have proposed several reforms that aim to reinvigorate parties in campaigns, which include raising or ending contribution limits to the parties as well as restrictions on party support to candidates, stronger limitations on donations that are sent directly to candidates, and public funds for parties.

Eliminating the debt ceiling, easing the rules to end a filibuster, improving judicial confirmations, and curbing the influence of private campaign dollars are four reforms that would facilitate a more responsible style of partisanship.

Regular Order

A second path to responsible partisanship would be to permanently restore "regular order." The breakdown of regular order has been a consequence of intensified partisanship while also being a barrier to responsible partisanship. Since the 1970s, the traditional decision-making processes have increasingly been circumvented. As party leaders took on a more forceful position in the chambers, fewer bills were handled by the traditional pathway: proposals first being considered by committees in hearings, then those proposals being marked up in executive session, and then those proposals debated on the floor with the possibility of being amended. According to the definition provided by the Congressional Research Service, "Regular order is generally viewed as a systematic, step-by-step lawmaking process that emphasizes the role of committees: bill introduction and referral to committee; the conduct of committee hearings, markups, and reports on legislation; House and Senate floor consideration of committee-reported measures; and the creation of conference committees to resolve bicameral differences."

Instead, the process became top heavy. In their efforts to maintain tight control over the body, both parties have relied on fast-track measures and limited input from the rank and file. Over time, the Speaker and Senate Majority Leader played a much bigger role in dictating the agenda and controlling the committees. There are fewer opportunities for regular members to affect deliberations. In the House, the Rules Committee became an extension of the leadership, with chairs attaching rules that were demanded by the party to ease passage. Once bills reached the floor, there were few opportunities to offer amendments.

Reestablishing regular order will require renewing some of the strength of committees that was lost in the 1970s and providing them with room to act more independently of leadership. Rule changes would have to allow for greater floor participation, including the ability to offer amendments. Conference committees would be restored as forums to resolve interchamber disputes. Congress should impose restrictions on the use of omnibus bills and reconciliation, if coupled with reductions in the cloture rules. Insisting that both parties can agree to abide by the constitutional requirement that there be a quorum to do business—a provision usually ignored as the House and Senate assume a quorum is present rather than really requiring it unless a member calls a point of order—would result in members spending more face-to-face time, a healthy antidote to the corrosive effects of the Tuesday-Thursday Club. Republicans should jettison the "Hastert Rule" to give greater opportunity for legislation that commands some Democratic support to be voted on in a Republican House.

To be sure, at one level there is clear tension between partisanship and regular order. Legislators in the 1980s and 1990s perceived these to be binary: either have strong parties where leaders control the process or have a decentralized system where committees and the rank and file sway decisions.

But just as reformers in the 1970s discerned that it was useful for strong, centralized parties to be held accountable and forced, through rules, to engage rank-and-file members, so, too, today we can see how both elements go hand in hand. Party leaders who lead relatively united caucuses and retain formidable tools to sway members can achieve greater buy-in among the rank and file for the decisions that they make. There have been moments in congressional history when party leaders were willing to enforce regular order and promote related norms. Regular order can help to push the leaders toward the kind of responsible model that limits despotic inclinations and strengthens confidence in the legitimacy of outcomes. The immediate costs of delegating power can pay off if the standing of the decisions party leaders do make, including some of the most difficult trade-offs, carry greater weight among colleagues. By reestablishing regular order, party leaders can walk away from victory with the losers feeling that the rules shaping deliberations had been fair and that they would be again next time the matter was debated.

Moving in the other direction, the House should restore the 2019 reform that raised the threshold required to put forth a motion to vacate the Speakership. Going back to the rules that the House temporarily adhered to during the short window, with a majority of one party having to back the resolution, would offer a slight improvement by granting party leaders a bit more space to make difficult decisions that are in the interest of the nation but not necessarily acceptable to everyone in the party.

Partisan Integration

One powerful element of partisanship in the nineteenth century was that it was woven into a public culture that connected the white male electorate to the party institutions that represented them. Without romanticizing what drove citizens to participate in party activities, and recognizing the limitations of the franchise before 1965, political parties in the nineteenth century served an important intermediary function between citizens and the state. At the height of partisan tensions in the Gilded Age, rates of voting remained extremely high and parties were seen by citizens as a valuable institution in their lives.

In recent decades, we have experienced another era of intensified partisan conflict but with rising levels of distrust of and disconnection from the democratic process. The result, argues political scientist Julia Azari, has been "weak parties and strong partisanship." The disillusionment born out of Vietnam and Watergate never disappeared. The reinvigorated partisanship after the 1960s was layered over this sentiment. Even worse, the structure of contemporary party organizations is too top heavy. Voters tend to feel strong attachment to their party despite these institutions being largely absent from daily lives filled up with consumption, work, and family. "Hollow parties," as Daniel Schlozman and Sam Rosenfeld have argued, "are unrooted in communities and unfelt in ordinary people's day-to-day-lives." It is for this reason that so many Americans are passionate about Democrats and Republicans but barely encounter party officials or participate in party activities outside of receiving solicitation texts, watching television, or scrolling through social media advertisements. Under these conditions, parties no longer serve the function of forging connective tissue that helps maintain faith in the democratic process.

Reforms to achieve responsible partisanship must create mechanisms that foster serious engagement by citizens in political activity. The goal should be to reduce the distance between the voter and the legislator. Improved communication between members and voters will be a place to start. Some localities have been exploring changes to the town hall format, an important component for national representatives and senators, to make them less imposing and dominated by activists. Some of the innovations have included the use of high-quality livestreaming platforms, along with breakout sessions online and in person, to encourage dialogue. Having members commit to a minimum of four digital town hall meetings per year or citizen boards focused on specialized issues can entrench these interactions. Another recent innovation has been to assemble "citizens' assemblies," where citizens are brought together around specific issues, such as the debt or criminal justice, and have submitted recommendations to congresspersons. During the run-up to midterms, there have been several moments, such as with the Tea Party in 2010 and the Democratic anti-Trump vote in 2018, when the party apparatus demonstrated the clear capacity to forge meaningful connections with frustrated voters.

Although the campaign finance laws that promoted party-building activity in the 1980s and 1990s—called "soft money"—proved to be extremely problematic as they were enacted and regulated, the basic goal of that system still has immense value. If there can be government incentives for disclosed donations that actually help cover the expenses of local party-directed initiatives, with certain kinds of projects specified, such reforms could foster citizen engagement with the party. More funding, for example, can be devoted to support parties developing promotional and recruitment initiatives that target constituencies, such as younger voters and poor Black Americans, to participate in door-to-door canvassing, phone banks, or poll watching.

In the *Columbia Law Review,* Tabatha Abu El-Haj and Didi Kuo have labeled such efforts "associational party-building." These law scholars pointed to recent developments showing what can be achieved. El-Haj and Kuo looked at measures that were recently implemented by both parties to boost participation. Indiana Republican Jim Banks proposed having members of the caucus convene specialized roundtables organized around particular occupations such as janitor, electrician, and restaurant owner. Texas and Nevada Democrats have put resources into in-person canvassing operations and multilingual hotlines, as well as celebratory events targeting ethnic groups. Nevada Republicans undertook efforts that included debate-watching parties and game-night fundraisers. Expanding on these initiatives would require substantial investments in state and local parties, given that only they have the true capacity to serve as full-time intermediary institutions. Engaging in these kinds of operations, the authors argue, benefits the parties as well at the electoral level: "Parties were stronger where they canvassed door-to-door and worked through peer and local civic networks."

The protection of voting rights must be at the heart of effective partisan integration. The past decades have seen a steady erosion of the Voting Rights Act of 1965. After the Supreme Court knocked down the key provision of the law in *Shelby v. Holder* (2013), red states have passed large numbers of bills imposing new restrictions on the vote. Restoring the VRA and dismantling the new limitations would make voting easier, more inviting, and less intimidating. The more that people become engaged in the act of voting, feeling a stake in elections, the stronger their attachments will become to the party system as agents, not just spectators, in political change.

Expanding the size of the House of Representatives would be a key step toward creating an integrative style of responsible partisanship that is more representative and responsive to the population. The House has been stuck at 435 members for far too long. It has remained the same size since Woodrow Wilson's first term. The total number was locked in in 1929 when the House passed the Permanent Apportionment Act, which instituted a formula for apportioning the 435 seats. Despite the fact that the population has more than doubled since that time, the composition of the House has not changed. The average district had reached 740,000 by 2015, a dramatic rise from the 300,000 in 1940. This contradicts what the founders, who clearly wanted the House to grow along with the population, envisioned in the Constitution.

Districts have grown too large, which creates a number of significant problems that curtail the ability of legislators to have genuine interactions with voters. Even in the age of computers and Zoom meetings, it remains difficult for most members to engage in meaningful contact with large swaths of their constituency. No matter how much time a member allocates to traveling back home to meet with voters, there are too many people to see and too many organizations to interact with—and too many groups to raise money from. As a result, members are more likely to hear from the most active and the most vocal persons in their specific electorate, thereby replicating the same kind of dynamics that occur in primaries and caucuses.

An added benefit of expanding the House, as political theorist Danielle Allen argued, would be to counterbalance some of the problems caused by the Electoral College. Our system for picking presidents has come under considerable criticism because the Electoral College favors smaller states, which already benefit from the anti-majoritarian structure of the Senate. Expanding the size of the House would allow the lower chamber to fulfill its obligation of offering proper representation to populous states. "A larger House of Representatives will reduce the advantage of small states to an appropriate level," offering some counterbalance to the Senate and Electoral College. At a practical level, as Allen confirmed in discussions with top architects, it would be feasible to renovate the physical infrastructure of the House and adjacent office buildings—as has been done many times—to facilitate additional members.

Strong partisanship benefits citizen engagement. The more that politicians and the electorate maintain grassroots ties, the more enduring the roots that bind the party organization together will be.

Normative Leadership

In the end, procedural and organizational reforms won't be sufficient. If we have learned anything in recent years, it is that leadership matters a great deal in shaping the direction of politics, more so than many earlier generations of reformers realized. In the moments of American history when norms have broken down among leaders, such as in Congress in the decade leading up to the Civil War, the results have been violence and chaos. To reestablish broken norms, courageous leadership will be essential and it will mean swimming against the currents of Washington. Congress needs elected officials who embrace partisanship but demonstrate that the quest for power must not overwhelm all other obligations.

Over the years, much of the literature about leadership has hinged on a debate between two different models: transformational and transactional. According to this scholarly work, *transformational leadership* has been exhibited by presidents such as

Franklin Roosevelt and Ronald Reagan. These have been leaders who have been able to push for and legitimize fundamentally new ideas and to create enduring coalitions. *Transactional leaders* are different. In the realm of the presidency, they included figures such as Presidents Truman and Clinton, who proved to be enormously effective at working within the coalitional and ideational context that they inherited but then concentrated on translating ideas into programmatic results. According to James MacGregor Burns, who spent much of his career after publishing *Deadlock of Democracy* writing about leadership, there were important differences between the styles: "If the *transactions* between leaders and followers result in realizing the individual goals of each, followers may satisfy certain wants, such as food or drink, in order to realize goals higher in the hierarchy of values, such as aesthetic needs. The chief monitors of transactional leadership are *modal values,* that is, values of means—honesty, responsibility, fairness, the honoring of commitments—without which transactional leadership could not work. Transformational leadership is more concerned with *end-values,* such as liberty, justice, equality. Transforming leaders 'raise' their followers up through levels of morality, though insufficient attention to means can corrupt the ends."

Transformative and transactional leadership are both vital, but to achieve responsible partisanship we will need bold individuals who exhibit *normative leadership*. These will include elected officials who demonstrate through action how to balance the imperatives of partisan politics with governance and the protection of democratic institutions. They will have to devote political capital to reestablishing norms that have been abandoned. As role models, they can demonstrate how a politician can respect guardrails while still thriving. In many respects, this is the model that Biden has tried to promote for the presidency. Even his withdrawal from the 2024 presidential campaign will symbolize how a politician can act for party and country rather than for self-interest and the preservation of power.

As Utah governor Spencer Cox, chair of the National Governors Association and a solidly conservative Republican, said in his address to colleagues, elected officials need to learn how to "disagree better." Normative leadership is integral to building effective parties that can offer the crucial gatekeeping function Levitsky and Ziblatt wrote about, while remaining powerful forces over Capitol Hill and without re-creating the anti-democratic tendencies of the pre-1970s system.

Politicians have the capacity to check some of the damaging hyperpartisanship in the public culture by pushing back against the dynamics of institutions such as social media. If more politicians would refuse to spread and reject disinformation, the political scientist Adam Berinsky argues, they can have an effect on checking the flow that comes out of our smartphones and tablets.

We have even seen a few glimmers of potential change within the highly radicalized GOP. At the height of the 2020 election crisis, Vice President Mike Pence refused to go along with the president's pressure to overturn the election. In Georgia, Secretary of State Brad Raffensperger and Governor Brian Kemp rebuffed Trump's fishing expedition for votes in their state. The following year, Wyoming Republican Liz Cheney, a staunch conservative, joined a handful of colleagues, including Illinois Republican Adam Kinzinger, in conducting a major investigation despite the high costs to their own careers. Of course, what they did should have been a commonsense expectation. Nonetheless, these examples from a radicalized Republican Party offer glimmers of hope that a different course of politics is possible.

Reforms to the presidential nomination process would be useful in improving the chances for better leadership at the very top, which would redound to the benefit of the party caucuses in Congress. Modifying the process put into place following 1968 could strengthen the role of party officials at the national convention to regain some influence over scrutinizing the values, ethics, and governing skills of future presidents. Without undermining the ability of voters to drive the decision in primaries and caucuses, a modified system that restores some substantive role for party officials (who would be much more diverse than in yesteryear) could enhance the ability of the parties to check candidates who would fuel destructive, as opposed to responsible, partisanship. In 1984, Democrats demonstrated how such reforms have an impact with the introduction of superdelegates, senior politicians, DNC members, and elected officials free to vote as they wish, whose votes have helped contain some of the destabilizing dynamics at work within the GOP.

Reform is a marathon, not a sprint. And the marathon will be even more difficult given the damage that Trump has inflicted in his campaign to discredit democratic institutions, including the parties. The process begins with an incubation period, as Nelson Polsby once called the earliest stages of policymaking, as thinkers and politicians must devote time to discussing, debating, refining, and testing proposals for reform. The next stage requires politicians sympathetic to improving our democracy—as well as nonpolitical actors within institutions such as the newsroom—to float ideas, deliberate over concrete proposals, and encourage vigorous debate. Reforms should be refined and adjusted. When another window of opportunity opens, as occurred in the Progressive Era and the 1970s, the groundwork for moving forward with programmatic change must be laid to maximize the odds of success. Previous windows have been opened as a result of major crises and scandals.

The time has come for bold thinking in American politics. The tremendous instabilities that currently exist within our democratic system have created a moment comparable to earlier periods of major reform. We are now in one of these periods. The chaos that surrounded the 2020 presidential election was part of a global movement of autocratic forces that has destabilized our democracy. It did not come from nowhere. The United States has been falling in terms of how the Freedom House Global Freedom Index grades the health of democracies (declining from 90 in 2015 to 83 in 2021).

Addressing the causes underlying the democratic backsliding will require doing more than punishing the perpetrators of January 6 and patching the glitches in the Electoral College, both of which are important. Saving ourselves from decline will necessitate tackling the dangerous dysfunctions that our hyperpartisanship has produced—without gutting the parties of the tremendous potential they continue to hold for providing Americans a legitimate pathway to debate, negotiate, and legislate solutions to the serious ideological differences that separate us.

If we don't alter course in the near future, we will keep dividing ourselves to death. Reformers need to put their time and energy into crafting a better kind of partisanship, one that is not totalizing and where the leadership accepts restraint. Not only is this agenda for reform feasible but it embraces and respects the promise that responsible parties continue to offer our democratic system.

The stakes are high. There needs to be stable rules in place bounding party competition. If such reforms happen, the nation can build a political system that is more responsive to national problems while offering voters real choices as to who should fight for their ideas as the debates on Capitol Hill unfold. If reformers can reconstitute the way that Democrats and Republicans work, the path to a healthier democracy via responsible partisanship is within our grasp. If reformers fail, the future will be bleak.

ACKNOWLEDGMENTS

This book is the culmination of many years of learning, writing, and teaching about the history of our democratic system. The findings rest on the shoulders of so many intellectual giants who have taught me in the classroom—such as the person to whom this book is dedicated, Morton Keller—through their books and lectures, and as colleagues participating in conferences and seminars. I have been a lucky student.

In Defense of Partisanship was born out of a delightful lunch at the Century Association in New York City with my friend Robert McDuffie, a brilliant violinist. Over the course of a meal, talking about music, family, and politics, Bobby mentioned that his wife, Camille, worked as the publisher for the Global Reports series. I knew about the series through the editor and founder, Nicholas Lemann, who had shown me a few copies over dinner a few weeks earlier. Bobby asked what my dream book would be if I decided to contribute to the series. The question stuck. At a holiday party in their apartment a few weeks later, I mentioned to Camille and Nick that I would be interested in doing something for the series if there was ever an opportunity, which then triggered a series of conversations culminating in this book. Thanks also to my dear friend Robert Caro. While I was deciding whether or not to tackle this project, he strongly encouraged me to undertake the challenge given the kinds of contributions he believes I offer to our public dialogue about American politics. His enthusiastic words of support always mean the world to me.

The entire publication process has been superb. Nick, along with Camille and Jimmy So, are a formidable CGR team who helped me conceive of the project and offered ongoing editorial support. Jaime Leifer has provided a smooth transition after Camille retired. The list of authors who compose this series are some of the most interesting minds in the media and academia. Brad Schwartz, a talented writer and doctoral student, provided outstanding research assistance helping me track down some key quotations. Jake Blumgart helped me fact-check and Madeleine Adams provided some editorial assistance.

Tim Duggan, the executive editor of Henry Holt, a good friend and fellow Centurion, provided sage advice in thinking through the project. Over cocktails, he offered me the perfect elevator pitch for this book. Thanks to the generous Sid Lapidus and Michael Weisberg, who funded a fellowship at the New York Historical Society, arranged by the brilliant director Louise Mirrer, which gave me time to write this book. Moreover, Dean Amaney Jamal at Princeton School of Public and International Affairs (SPIA) ensured that everything was in place so I could take a full year of leave from Princeton to work on this and another major project.

Thanks to my wonderful colleague Frances Lee at Princeton for reading an earlier draft of the manuscript and providing valuable editorial suggestions. Frances is one of the world's most insightful scholars of Congress. Although we don't always reach the same conclusions, I learn from her analysis of our treasured democratic institution. Gary Gerstle, my fellow coeditor at Princeton University, has always been a model to me for how historians can synthesize vast amounts of scholarship into original arguments of their own—work that helps to make sense of disparate pieces. He proved an extremely insightful reader, who made this a better book. Finally, I want to thank Sarah Binder for her editorial comments. Sarah is a formidable scholar and friend whose work has continued to influence me since we met at Brookings, and her reading was enormously valuable. And Jack Rakove generously helped me work through a few questions about James Madison.

My family provided unending support and love as I worked my way through this project. My parents, Jerry and Viviana, continue to offer unconditional support and enthusiasm. While completing work on this book, my mother-in-law, Eleanore Jacobs, passed away. I will forever be grateful to the way that Ellie welcomed me into the family and treated our kids with such love. I imagine that somewhere in heaven it's five o'clock, and she is sitting with a vodka in one hand and with the other holding her love, the late Arthur Jacobs, as he enjoys this book. My wife, Meg, as she worked on her own important book about the New Deal and World War II, found time to graciously read the manuscript and offered wonderful suggestions about how to bring out some of the history. Meg has been the perfect partner and built us a new home in New York that is simply magnificent. The adventure we have undertaken together continues to inspire and energize. Our four kids, Abigail, Sophia, Nathan, and Claire, provide an endless source of joy. Watching them learn the world as college students, walking away with interpretations of their own, gives me great pride and hope, even in our difficult times, that the future will be bright.

FURTHER READING

The history of bipartisanship has been a fruitful area of exploration. Some of the best work has challenged the nostalgic understanding of what cross-partisan collaboration entailed between the 1930s and 1970s. See, for example, James Sundquist, *Politics and Policy: The Eisenhower, Kennedy, and Johnson Years* (Washington: Brookings, 1968); Ira Katznelson, *When Affirmative Action Was White: An Untold History of Racial Inequality in Twentieth -Century America* (New York: W. W. Norton & Company, 2005).

For a historical understanding of parties and procedure, see Sarah Binder, *Minority Rights, Majority Rule: Partisanship and the Development of Congress* (New York: Cambridge University Press, 1997); Eric Schickler, *Disjointed Pluralism: Institutional Innovation and the Development of the U.S. Congress* (Princeton: Princeton University Press, 2001); Gregory Wawro and Eric Schickler, *Filibuster: Obstruction and Lawmaking in the U.S. Senate* (Princeton: Princeton University Press, 2006).

There has been a vast body of social scientific literature focusing on the intensification of partisanship in American politics since the 1960s: See David W. Rohde, *Parties and Leaders in the Postreform House* (Chicago: University of Chicago Press, 1991); E.J. Dionne Jr., *Why Americans Hate Politics* (New York: Simon & Schuster, 1991); John Jacobs, *A Rage for Justice: The Passion and Politics of Phillip Burton* (Berkeley: University of California Press, 1997); Marcus Pryor, *Post-Broadcast Democracy: How Media Choice Increases Inequality in Political Involvement and Polarizes Elections* (New York: Cambridge University Press, 2007); Julian E. Zelizer, *On Capitol Hill: The Struggle to Reform Congress and Its Consequences, 1948–2000* (New York: Cambridge University Press, 2004); Juliet Eilperin, *Fight Club Politics: How Partisanship Is Poisoning the House of Representatives* (New York: Rowan Littlefield, 2007); Ronald Brownstein, *The Second Civil War: How Extreme Polarization Has Paralyzed Washington and Polarized America* (New York: Penguin, 2007); Thomas Mann and Norman J. Ornstein, *It's Even Worse Than it Looks: How the American Constitutional System Collided with the New Politics of Extremism* (New York: Basic Books, 2012); Sam Rosenfeld, *The Polarizers: Postwar Architects of Our Partisan Era* (Chicago: University of Chicago Press, 2017); John Lawrence, *The Class of '74: Congress After Watergate and the Roots of Partisanship* (Baltimore: Johns Hopkins University Press, 2018); Steve Kornacki, *The Red and the Blue: The 1990s and the Birth of Political Tribalism* (New York: Ecco, 2018).

Finally, a number of thoughtful recent books have evaluated the impact of partisanship in current times. See Frances E. Lee, *Insecure Majorities: Congress and the Perpetual Campaign* (Chicago: University of Chicago

Press, 2016); Matt Grossman and David A. Hopkins, *Asymmetric Politics: Ideological Republicans and Group Interest Democrats* (New York: Oxford University Press, 2016); James M. Curry and Frances Lee, *The Limits of Party: Congress and Lawmaking in a Polarized Era* (Chicago: University of Chicago Press, 2020); Ezra Klein, *Why We Are Polarized* (New York: Simon & Schuster, 2020).

NOTES

CHAPTER ONE

12 **warns of Washington's toxic environment:** Chris Matthews, *Tip and Gipper: When Politics Worked* (New York: Simon & Schuster, 2013).

12 **that we were amusing ourselves to death with television:** Neil Postman, *Amusing Ourselves to Death,* revised ed. (New York: Penguin Press, 2005).

12 **we are tearing ourselves apart through partisanship:** Steve S. Smith, Jason M. Roberts, and Ryan J. Vander Wielen, *The American Congress, 9th ed.* (New York: Cambridge, 2015), 57.

13 **"Yes, Larry, I'm a Republican," she says:** "Opening Night," *Curb Your Enthusiasm,* Season 4, Episode 10.

13 **interpolitical marriages have become increasingly frowned upon:** Lynn Vavreck, "A Measure of Identity: Are You Wedded to Your Party?" *New York Times,* January 31, 2017.

14 **Lawmakers are themselves to blame:** Roger H. Davidson, Walter J. Oleszek, Frances E. Lee, and Eric Schickler, *Congress and Its Members,* 17th ed. (Washington: Sage and CQ Press, 2020), xxii.

14 **Madisonians count on the separation of powers, federalism, and bicameralism:** For two of the most thoughtful examples of this line of thinking, see Philip A. Wallach, *Why Congress* (New York: Oxford University Press, 2023), and David Mayhew, *America's Congress: Actions in the Public Sphere, James Madison Through Newt Gingrich* (New Haven, CT: Yale University Press, 2002).

15 **"common-sense majority":** Jonathan Weisman, "A Third-Party Soft Launches, but Its Politicians Disagree on Details," *New York Times,* July 17, 2023.

15 **procedural changes, such as removing party labels from ballots:** Adam Nagourney, "Bloomberg Says Elections Should Be Nonpartisan," *New York Times,* June 8, 2001.

15 **"You can find this distaste for faction and longing for unity":** Jamelle Bouie, "Joe Manchin Is Dreaming," *New York Times,* July 25, 2023.

17 **is perceived by this school to be a positive development:** Sidney M. Milkis, *The President and the Parties: The Transformation of the American Party System Since the New Deal* (New York: Oxford University Press, 1993).

17 **called the entire Constitution outdated:** William G. Howell and Terry M. Moe, *Relic: How Our Constitution Undermines Effective Government, and Why We Need a*

More Powerful Presidency (New York: Basic Books, 2016).

19 **on foreign policy bipartisanship has still driven many policy decisions:** Jordan Tama, *Bipartisanship and US Foreign Policy: Cooperation in a Polarized Age* (New York: Oxford University Press, 2024). See also, on divided government, polarization, and domestic policymaking, James M. Curry and Frances Lee, *The Limits of Party: Congress and Lawmaking in a Polarized Era* (Chicago: University of Chicago, 2020).

19 **There are issues where significant blocs of one party break with the leadership:** David Leonhardt, "A New Centrism Is Rising in Washington," *New York Times*, May 19, 2024.

19 **have been able to offer voters distinct ideological visions throughout American history:** John Gerring, *Party Ideologies in America, 1828–1996* (New York: Cambridge University Press, 1998).

20 **parties can organize, simplify, sort, and explain these quandaries:** Seth Masket and Hans Noel, *Political Parties* (New York: W. W. Norton & Company, 2021), 7.

20–21 **until the 1960s depended on closed, smoke-filled rooms that were not very democratic:** Steven Levitsky and Daniel Ziblatt, *How Democracies Die: What History Tells Us About Our Future* (New York: Crown, 2018), 36–37; 96–118.

21 **where the factions and interests of our polity attempt to work out compromises:** Philip A. Wallach, *Why Congress*.

CHAPTER TWO

22 **"break and control the violence of faction":** James Madison, *Federalist* 10, 1787.

23 **disinterested and independent leaders who could not be corrupted:** Richard Hofstadter, *The Idea of a Party System: The Rise of Legitimate Opposition in the United States, 1780–1840* (Berkeley: University of California Press, 1969), xii; Gordon S. Wood, *The Radicalism of the American Revolution: How a Revolution Transformed a Monarchical Society into a Democratic One Unlike Any That Had Ever Existed* (New York: Knopf, 1992), 253–254.

23 **"had become its ability to control factions":** Gordon S. Wood, *The Creation of the American Republic, 1776–1787* (New York: W. W. Norton & Company, 1969), 502.

23 **in such a way as to reduce this threat:** Jack N. Rakove, *A Politician Thinking: The Creative Mind of James Madison* (Norman: University of Oklahoma Press, 2017), 86.

23 **in contrast to conceptions of small and homogeneous republics:** On the fears of direct democracy, see Bernard Bailyn, *The Ideological Origins of the American Revolution* (Belknap, MA: The Belknap Press of Harvard University Press, 1992), 282–83.

24 **"worst enemy" of democracy:** James Sundquist, *Politics and Policy: The Eisenhower, Kennedy, and Johnson Years* (Washington: Brookings, 1968), 495.

24 **"is to be dreaded as the great political evil":** George Washington, "Farewell Address," September 19, 1796.

24 **justifying his decision as necessary to save Republicanism:** Noah Feldman, *The Three Lives of James Madison: Genius, Partisan, President* (New York: Random House, 2017), 347; Richard Brookshiser, *James Madison* (New York: Basic Books, 2011), 98–99.

24 **"We must always have party distinctions":** Martin Van Buren to Thomas Ritchie, 1827, in Ronald E. Elkins, ed., *The Evolution of Political Parties, Campaigns and Elections, Landmark Documents, 1787–2007* (Washington, DC: CQ Press, 2008), 67–68.

25 **envisioned the organizational potential of parties:** Ted Widmer, *Martin Van Buren* (New York: Times Books, 2005), 56–57.

25 **"an evil inherent in free government":** Alexis de Tocqueville, *Democracy in America* (New York: Harper, 1969), 174–75.

25 **essential organizational mechanisms for parties as institutions:** Joel H. Silbey, *The American Political Nation: 1838–1893* (Palo Alto, CA: Stanford University Press, 1994), 45, 128.

25 **Religious, economic, and, to some extent, sectional identities:** Ronald P. Formisano, "The 'Party Period' Revisited," *Journal of American History* 86, no. 1 (June 1999): 93–120; Formisano, *The Birth of Mass Political Parties: Michigan, 1827–1861* (Princeton, NJ: Princeton University Press, 1971); Alan Bogue, "United States: The New 'Political History,'" *Journal of Contemporary History* 3, no. 1 (January 1968): 5–27; Paul Kleppner, *The Cross of Culture: A Social Analysis of Midwestern Politics 1850–1900* (New York: Free Press, 1970); J. Morgan Kousser, "The 'New Political History': A Methodological Critique," *Reviews in American History* 4, no. 1 (March 1976): 1–14.

25 **breaking up policy and oversight jurisdiction into panels:** Roger H. Davidson, Walter J. Oleszek, Frances E. Lee, and Eric Schickler, *Congress and Its Members*, 178.

26 **they more than doubled by the time he was finished in 1825:** Sean M. Theriault and Mickey Edwards, *Congress: The First Branch* (New York: Oxford University Press, 2020), 212–13.

26 **provided them the best opportunity to influence final legislative outcomes:** Charles Stewart III, *Analyzing Congress: The New Institutionalism in American Politics*, 2nd ed. (New York: W. W. Norton & Company, 2012), 105–6.

26 **physical violence, which became a regular occurrence on the floors of Congress:** Joanne Freeman, *The Field of Blood: Violence in Congress and the Road to Civil War* (New York: Farrar, Straus and Giroux, 2018).

27 **anti-partyism:** Rachel A. Shelden and Erik B. Alexander, "Dismantling the Party System: Party Fluidity and the Mechanisms of Nineteenth-Century U.S. Politics," *Journal of American History* (December 2023): 419–48.

27 **aimed to remake the South by working with freed slaves:** Eric Foner, *Reconstruction: America's Unfinished Revolution, 1863–1877* (New York: HarperCollins, 1988).

28 **looked to economic and regulatory policies as a way to move beyond some of the fractures:** Richard Bensel, *The Political Economy of American Industrialization, 1877–1900* (New York: Cambridge University Press, 2000).

28 **became powerful forces in state and local government:** Joel H. Silbey, *The American Political Nation*, 45.

29 **political parties constituted the best way to assert popular control:** Austin Ranney, *The Doctrine of Responsible Party Government* (Urbana: University of Illinois Press, 1954), 11.

29 **began working out his ideas about how parties should function:** Ranney, *The Doctrine of Responsible Party Government*, 25–26.

30 **"our own peculiar and incomparable possession":** Woodrow Wilson, *Congressional Government: A Study in American Politics* (New York: Houghton Mifflin, 1885), 5.

31 **"We are ruled by a score and a half of 'little legislatures'":** Woodrow Wilson, *Congressional Government: A Study in American Politics*, 113.

31 **"the youngest clerk might rise even to the chief magistracy":** Woodrow Wilson, *Congressional Government: A Study in American Politics*, 254.

32 **"no *visible*, and therefore no *controllable* party organization":** Woodrow Wilson, *Congressional*

Government: A Study in American Politics, 33.

32 **as a flawed institution, it retained too much power over the president:** Jessica Korn, *The Power of Separation* (Princeton, NJ: Princeton University Press, 1996), 19.

32 **"exercise an almost despotic sway within their own shires":** Woodrow Wilson, *Congressional Government: A Study in American Politics,* 31.

33 **"what shall be done at those times when some decision there must be":** Woodrow Wilson, *Congressional Government: A Study in American Politics,* 89.

33 **"best rulers are always those to whom great power is entrusted in such a manner":** Woodrow Wilson, *Congressional Government: A Study in American Politics,* 89–90.

33 **"any common purpose in the measures which its Committees from time to time recommend":** Woodrow Wilson, *Congressional Government: A Study in American Politics,* 21.

33 **the same kinds of bureaucratic managerial structures:** Robert Wiebe, *The Search For Order, 1877–1920* (New York: Hill and Wang, 1967); Alfred Chandler, *The Visible Hand: The Managerial Revolution in American Business* (Cambridge, MA: Belknap Press, 1977).

34 **"began to transmute fact into law, law into fact":** Woodrow Wilson, "The Reconstruction of the Southern States," *The Atlantic* (January 1901): 12.For the best exploration of how Wilson's views on race intersected with his administration, see Eric S. Yellin, *Racism in the Nation's Service: Government Workers and the Color Line in Woodrow Wilson's America* (Chapel Hill: University of North Carolina, 2013).

35 **"to follow blindly the political party which had brought on the war of their emancipation":** Woodrow Wilson, *A History of the American People, Vol. V,* revised ed. (New York: Cosimo Classics, 2008), 18, 46.

35 **"not covertly and on the sly":** Woodrow Wilson, *Congressional Government: A Study in American Politics,* 108, 114.

36 **refusal to appreciate the dangers of majoritarianism:** John Milton Cooper, *Woodrow Wilson: A Biography* (New York: Vintage, 2011), 50.

36 **articulated similar themes:** James Bryce, *American Commonwealth* (New York: MacMillan, 1889); A. Lawrence Lowell, *Essays on Government* (Boston: Houghton Mifflin, 1889), Frank Goodnow, *Politics and Administration: A Study in*

Government (New York: MacMillan, 1914).

36 **"Cursing, drinking, sometimes fighting":** Steven Hahn, *Illiberal America: A History* (New York: W. W. Norton & Company, 2024), 122–23. For the best history of the limits of what drove Americans to these events, see Glenn C. Altschuler and Stuart M. Blumin, *Rude Republic: Americans and Their Politics in the Nineteenth Century* (Princeton, NJ: Princeton University Press, 2000).

36–37 **Party newspapers were the main source for information:** Michael McGerr, *The Decline of Popular Politics: The American North, 1865–1928* (New York: Oxford University Press, 1986).

37 **taught children about the importance of parties:** Jean Baker, *Affairs of Party: The Political Culture of Northern Democrats in Mid-Nineteenth Century* (New York: Fordham Press, 1998).

37 **"were awash in the most bitter and intense partisan rhetoric":** Joel H. Silbey, "Congress in a Partisan Political Era," in *The American Congress: The Building of Democracy*, ed. Julian E. Zelizer (Boston: Houghton Mifflin, 2004), 149. See also Joel H. Silbey, *The American Political Nation*; Nolan McCarty, Keith T. Poole, and Howard Rosenthal, *Polarized America: The Dance of Ideology and Unequal Riches,* 2nd ed. (Cambridge, MA: MIT Press, 2016).

37 **"the worst tyrant that ever ruled over a deliberative body":** Eric Rauchway, "The Transformation of the Congressional Experience," in *The American Congress,* 226–27.

38 **others focused on national policies to regulate food safety, child labor, and trusts:** See Daniel Rodgers, *Atlantic Crossings: Social Politics in a Progressive Age* (Cambridge, MA: Belknap Press of Harvard University Press, 1998), and Rodgers, "In Search of Progressivism," *Reviews in American History* 10, no. 4 (1982): 113–32.

38 **"by a mischievous, artificial and irresponsible method of representation":** Herbert Croly, *Progressive Democracy* (New York: Macmillan, 1914), 347–49.

39 **generated a backlash against federal programs:** Theda Skocpol, *Protecting Soldiers and Mothers: The Political Origins of Social Policy in the United States* (Cambridge, MA: Harvard University Press, 1995).

39 **were also aimed at making the franchise more cumbersome for working-class:** Hahn, *Illiberal America*, 190.

39 **"spokesman for the real sentiment and purpose of the country":** Woodrow Wilson,

Constitutional Government in the United States (New York: Columbia University Press, 1908), 67–69. For a discussion of his new views on the presidency, see John Milton Cooper Jr., *Woodrow Wilson: A Biography* (New York: Knopf, 2009).

40 **survived as major institutions in American politics:** Stephen Skowronek, *Building a New American State: The Expansion of National Administrative Capacities, 1877–1920* (New York: Cambridge University Press, 1982).

40 **progressivism did not slay the party dragon:** Morton Keller, *Affairs of State: Public Life in Late Nineteenth- Century America* (Cambridge, MA: Harvard University Press, 1977); Stephen Skowronek, *Building a New American State.*

41 **granted state and local governments discretion in implementing:** Robert C. Lieberman, *Shifting the Color Line: Race and the American Welfare State* (Cambridge, MA: Harvard University Press, 1998); Ira Katznelson, *When Affirmative Action Was White: An Untold History of Racial Inequality in Twentieth Century America* (New York: W. W. Norton & Company, 2005).

41 **"so long as it continues to be the party of militant liberalism":** President Franklin D. Roosevelt, *The Public Papers and Addresses of Franklin D. Roosevelt, 1938* vol., *The Continuing Struggle for Liberalism* (New York: MacMillan Company, 1941), xxxi.

42 **"have different names but are as alike in their principles":** President Franklin Roosevelt, Fireside Chat, "On Purging the Democratic Party," June 24, 1938, University of Virginia, Miller Center, Presidential Speeches Collection.

42 **fear of Roosevelt often overcame Dixiecrats' reluctance:** James T. Patterson, "A Conservative Coalition Forms in Congress," *Journal of American History* 52, no. 4 (March 1966): 769.

43 **"one liberal and the other conservative":** Susan Dunn, *Roosevelt's Purge: How FDR Fought to Change the Democratic Party* (Cambridge, MA: Belknap, 2010), 231–32.

43 **"be classified as belonging to the liberal school of thought":** Susan Dunn, *Roosevelt's Purge*, 162.

43 **"a time when I would have bled and died for him":** Julian E. Zelizer, *On Capitol Hill: The Struggle to Reform Congress and Its Consequences, 1948–2000* (New York: Cambridge University Press, 2004), 27–28.

44 **without much interaction with other Democrats:** Sidney Milkis, *The President and the Parties:*

The Transformation of the American Party System Since the New Deal (New York: Oxford University Press, 1993).

44 **removed from the legislative realm and thereby muted:** John J. Coleman, *Party Decline in America: Policy, Politics, and the Fiscal State* (Princeton, NJ: Princeton University Press, 1996).

45 **"Are you going to be a player":** "Bob Michel, Last Leader of the 'Old School' House GOP, Dies at 93," *Roll Call*, February 17, 2017.

45 **highest levels of bipartisan roll calls:** Nolan McCarty, Keith T. Poole, and Howard Rosenthal, *Polarized America*.

46 **"Negroes are not in a mood to accept lip service":** "Negro Group Asks Ban on Filibuster," *New York Times*, January 26, 1949.

46 **was stifling majoritarian demands:** Political scientists have long debated whether this was true, a counterfactual that will always be impossible to fully evaluate. Some have argued that liberals did not have a majority in the House before the Great Society that would be necessary for moving the legislation that came to be known as the Great Society.

46 **"we have given strength to the totalitarian forces":** Hubert Humphrey Papers, Minnesota Historical Society.

47 **"oxcart in the age of the atom":** Julian E. Zelizer, *On Capitol Hill*, 30.

47 **there were three different components to parties:** V. O. Key, *Politics, Parties, and Pressure Groups* (New York: Crowell, 1947).

47 **it is the party that casts a web:** V. O. Key, *Politics, Parties, and Pressure Groups*, 656.

48 **the two-party system moderated politics rather than inflaming passions:** E. E. Schattschneider, *Party Government: American Government in Action*, updated ed. (London: Routledge, 2004), 2–3; 85–93; 141; 193; 208–9. See also, E. E. Schattschneider, "Pressure Groups Versus Political Parties," *The Annals of the American Academy of Political and Social Science* 259 (September 1948): 18–19.

48 **existing two-party system, centered around the president, more robust:** Daniel Stid, "Two Pathways for Congressional Reform," The William and Flora Hewlett Foundation, March 11, 2015.

49 **deep dive into how these organizations could be improved:** John Morris, "Reform Is Urged in 2 Major Parties," *New York Times*, October 14, 1950.

49 **was the main author:** Sam Rosenfeld, *The Polarizers: Postwar*

Architects of Our Partisan Era (Chicago: University of Chicago Press, 2017), 15.

51 **through informal norms and personal relations:** Roger H. Davidson, David Kovenach, and Michael O'Leary, *Congress in Crisis: Politics and Congressional Reform* (San Francisco: Wadsworth, 1966), 144–45.

51 **a bipartisan establishment ruled:** William S. White, *The Citadel: The Story of the U.S. Senate* (New York: Harper, 1957).

51 **was needed to win reelection:** David Mayhew, *Congress: The Electoral Connection* (New Haven, CT: Yale University Press, 1974).

52 **What could be good for a Senator running for reelection:** Charles O. Jones, "Presidential Leadership in a Government of Parties," in *Responsible Partisanship? The Evolution of American Political Parties Since 1950*, eds. John C. Green and Paul S. Herring (Lawrence: University Press of Kansas, 2002), 141–59.

53 **why the existing party system had endured for so long:** Austin Ranney, "Toward a More Responsible Two-Party System: A Commentary," *American Political Science Review* 45, no. 2 (June 1951): 488–99.

54 **assumption that majority rule was always better:** Austin Ranney, *The Doctrine of Responsible Party Government*, 160–62.

54 **conflict between interest groups produced a level of stability:** David B. Truman, "The Politics of the New Collectivism," in *Trends in Modern American Society*, ed. Clarence Morris (Philadelphia: University of Pennsylvania Press, 1962), 130–31.

55 **"can be traced to the weakness of such consensus":** David B. Truman, "The American System in Crisis," *Political Science Quarterly* 74, no. 4 (December 1959): 481–97.

55 **would destabilize the equilibrium:** Murray S. Stedman Jr. and Herbert Sonthoff, "Party Responsibility—A Critical Inquiry," *Western Political Quarterly* 4, no.3 (September 1951): 466–67.

55 **worked well within the pluralists' favored framework:** David B. Truman, *The Governmental Process* (New York: Knopf, 1951).

55 **"You're Not Going to Ride on That Thing Around Here":** Jim Berryman, Cartoon, "You're Not Going to Ride on That Thing Around Here," *Washington Star*, July 1959. National Archives, https://lbj.artifacts.archives.gov/objects/40217/youre-not-going-to-ride?ctx=4ef357192f213cc27d261bc69cd0866c116b1b99&idx=1.

55 **had made centralizing his party a top priority:** Sam Rosenfeld, *The Polarizers*.

55 **undermined Butler's efforts to create an advisory council:** Sean J. Savage, *JFK, LBJ, and the Democratic Party* (Albany, NY: SUNY Press, 2004), 32.

56 **"most elaborately organized 'party within a party'":** James Sundquist, *Politics and Policy: The Eisenhower, Kennedy, and Johnson Years*, 495.

56 **parties were engines of bold policy change in moments of crisis:** V. O. Key, *A Theory of Critical Elections, The Journal of Politics*, 17, 3–18; Walter Dean Burnham, *Critical Elections and the Mainsprings of American Politics* (New York: W. W. Norton & Company, 1971); David Brady, *Critical Elections and Congressional Policymaking* (Palo Alto, CA: Stanford University Press, 1988). For a powerful critique of this idea, see David Mayhew, *Electoral Realignments: A Critique of an American Genre* (New Haven, CT: Yale University Press, 2002).

57 **what he believed to be the two great issues of the day:** James MacGregor Burns, *The Deadlock of Democracy: Four-Party Politics in America* (New York: Prentice Hall, 1963), 5.

57 **combination of competitive party politics and strong executive leadership:** James MacGregor Burns, *The Deadlock of Democracy*, 8–46.

58 **"Madisonian Model" had produced four political parties:** James MacGregor Burns, *The Deadlock of Democracy*, 257–64.

59 **allied with parochial, conservative small-town rural leaders:** "The Four Parties," *Time*, January 18, 1963: 21–22.

59 **"we have been too late with too little":** James MacGregor Burns, *The Deadlock of Democracy*, 3.

59 **"until we unfreeze our minds":** James MacGregor Burns, *The Deadlock of Democracy*, 7.

60 **mandating four-year terms in the US House of Representatives:** James MacGregor Burns, *The Deadlock of Democracy*, 327–32.

60 **"their often-celebrated handiwork of checks and balances":** C. Van Woodward, "Review: The Deadlock of Democracy," *Commentary*, June 1963.

60 **"tell a popular new President what he *can* do":** Dennis H. Wrong, "Who's in Charge?" *New York Review of Books*, February 1, 1963.

60 **"and got bloodied up in the attempt":** "The Four Parties," *Time*, January 18, 1963: 21–22.

61 **delivered a blistering address on the floor:** Joseph Clark, *Congress: The Sapless Branch* (New York: Harper & Row, 1964), 19.

61 **"its creaky, antiquated machinery":** "'Uncreative,' 'Negative,' 'Smug'—Is This Today's U.S. Congress?" *Newsweek*, January 28, 1963: 22.

61 **"perhaps slightly to the left of Ivan the Terrible":** Richard Bolling, *House Out of Order* (New York: Dutton, 1965).

62 **the civil rights struggle elevated national party loyalty above regionalism:** Julian E. Zelizer, *Is This America? Reckoning with Racism at the 1964 Atlantic City Democratic Convention* (work-in-progress, under contract with W. W. Norton & Company); Sam Rosenfeld, *The Polarizers*, 112–13.

63 **"rules that now bind the United States Congress to inactivity, irresponsibility, and inefficiency":** Press Release, the Americans for Democratic Action, May 1964, Papers of the Americans for Democratic Action, Wisconsin Historical Society.

64 **a "revolution" taking place before his very eyes:** Stephen Bailey, *The New Congress* (New York: St. Martin's Press, 1966).

65 **"one-man veto on Medicare":** Julian E. Zelizer, *Taxing America: Wilbur D. Mills, Congress, and the State, 1945–1975* (New York: Cambridge University Press, 1998), 139.

66 **"an effective conservative coalition":** John D. Morris, "G.O.P. House Gains Beset Democrats," *New York Times*, November 10, 1966.

66 **"will block almost any program put forward by the Great Society":** Jim Scovel, "Republicans Make Big Gains in House; Dems Hold Control," *Newsday*, November 9, 1966.

67 **"lost its forward movement and its inner spirit":** Cited in Robert M. Collins, "The Economic Crisis of 1968 and the Waning of 'the American Century,'" *American Historical Review* 101, no. 2 (April 1996): 422.

68 **responsible parties as a response to the disillusionment:** David S. Broder, "The Party's Over," *The Atlantic*, March 1972. See also David Halberstam, *The Best and Brightest* (New York: Random House, 1972).

68 **APSA conducted another major project:** Roger H. Davidson, David Kovenach, and Michael O'Leary, *Congress in Crisis*.

68 **an alternate reform tradition within the profession:** Daniel Stid, "Two Pathways for Congressional Reform," The William and Flora Hewlett Foundation, March 11, 2015.

68 **"Congress relegated to a secondary level of power":** Roger H. Davidson, David Kovenach, and Michael O'Leary, *Congress in Crisis*, 13.

68 **It was not that these scholars didn't support reform:** Nelson Polsby, *Congress and the Presidency* (Englewood Cliffs, NJ: Prentice Hall, 1964); Ralph K. Huitt, "The Outsider in the Senate: An Alternative Role," *American Political Science Review* 55 (September 1961): 566–71; Donald R. Matthews, *U.S. Senators and Their World* (Chapel Hill: University of North Carolina Press, 1960).

69 **"although he may have the morals of a Mafia capo or the mind of a moron":** Richard Bolling, "The House," *Playboy*, November 1969.

70 **"for blunting and minimizing conflict at too high a cost":** Richard Hofstadter, *The Idea of a Party System: The Rise of Legitimate Opposition in the United States, 1780–1840* (Berkeley: University of California Press, 1969), xii.

CHAPTER THREE

71 **the nation continued to be dangerously fragmented:** David Broder, "The Party's Over," *The Atlantic*, March 1972. For a full elaboration of his argument, see *The Party's Over: The Failure of Politics in America* (New York: Harper & Row, 1972).

72 **binding primaries and caucuses would determine the outcome:** Byron Shafer, *Quiet Revolution: The Struggle for the Democratic Party and the Shaping of Post-Reform Politics* (New York: Russell Sage Foundation, 1983).

72 **party elites retained more power than commentators initially predicted:** Marty Cohen, David Karol, Hans Noel, John Zaller, *The Party Decides: Presidential Nominations Before and After Reform* (Chicago: University of Chicago Press, 2008); John Sides and Lynn Vaverick, *The Gamble: Choice and Chance in the 2012 Presidential Election* (Princeton, NJ: Princeton University Press, 2013).

72 **when Barack Obama defeated Hillary Clinton:** Elaine C. Kamarack, *Primary Politics: Everything You Need to Know About How America Nominates Its Presidential Candidates* (Washington, D.C.: Brookings, 2023).

73 **can produce legislative action that favors general over special interests:** Douglas Arnold, *The Logic of Congressional Action* (New

Haven, CT: Yale University Press, 1992), 60–87.

74 **to lobby, mobilize support, and communicate with members:** Julian E. Zelizer, *On Capitol Hill;* Sam Rosenfeld, *The Polarizers,* 162.

74 **norms that sometimes contradicted one another:** Eric Schickler, *Disjointed Pluralism: Institutional Innovation and the Development of the U.S. Congress* (Princeton, NJ: Princeton University Press, 2004).

75 **"backbenchers want to and should be able to pull the plug":** Frances McCall Rosenbluth and Ian Shapiro, *Responsible Parties: Saving Democracy from Itself* (New Haven, CT: Yale University Press, 2018), 114.

75 **"right to know" was becoming an increasingly popular reform:** Michael Schudson, *The Right to Know: Politics and the Culture of Transparency, 1945–1975* (Cambridge, MA: Harvard University Press, 2018), 112.

76 **providing more generous resources for the committee minority:** Walter Kravitz, "The Advent of the Modern Congress: The Legislative Reorganization Act of 1970," *Legislative Studies Quarterly* 15, no. 3 (August 1990): 378.

77 **"in fact . . . leaders and not just survivors":** "Seniority System Challenged in Both Houses," *Congressional Quarterly Almanac,* 1971.

77 **had been shifting since the 1958 midterm elections:** Barbara Sinclair, *The Transformation of the U.S. Senate* (Baltimore: Johns Hopkins University Press, 1989).

77 **"Mansfield has acted as the Senate's servant":** "The President; The 92nd Congress," *Newsweek,* January 25, 1971: 16–21.

77 **"outmoded and improper for a twentieth century Congress":** John W. Finney, "Senate's Leaders Approve Reforms," *New York Times,* January 20, 1971.

78 **not only vindicated but triumphant:** James Reston, "Victory, 10 Years Later: Spectacular Nixon Vote Considered," *New York Times,* November 8, 1972.

78 **"the Supreme Court will be castrated":** Gary Wills, "Four More Years? Learning to Live with Nixon," *New York Times,* November 5, 1972.

79 **"whiff of Cannonism to them":** "Uncle Joe Cannon: 'Iron Duke' of Congress, *Time,* January 15, 1973: 13.

79 **"those lost powers were once taken for granted":** "The Crack in the Constitution," *Time,* January 15, 1973: 12.

80 **overwhelmed the traditional separation of powers:** Arthur M. Schlesinger Jr., *The Imperial Presidency* (Boston: Houghton Mifflin 1973), 208.

80 **"restraints could be introduced while preserving the best features of the presidency":** Leroy N. Rieselbach, "In the Wake of Watergate: Congressional Reform?" *Review of Politics* 36, no. 3 (July 1974): 371.

81 **"Presidents were objects of respect but not of veneration":** Arthur M. Schlesinger Jr., *The Imperial Presidency*, 208–11.

81 **was seen as a major step away from seniority:** Marjorie Hunter, "House Democrats Given Vote on Committee Heads," *New York Times*, January 23, 1973.

81 **"reminder to the chairmen that they are creatures of the Caucus":** John Lawrence, *The Class of '74: Congress After Watergate and the Roots of Partisanship* (Baltimore: Johns Hopkins University Press, 2018), 33.

82 **"would be required to run the gauntlet of the party caucus":** Sara Brandes Crook and John R. Hibbing, "Congressional Reform and Party Discipline: The Effects of Changes in the Seniority System on Party Loyalty in the US House of Representatives," *British Journal of Political Science* 15, no. 2 (April 1985): 209. Besides Eric Schickler, *Disjointed Pluralism*, two excellent books that examine the reforms of the 1970s are David W. Rohde, *Parties and Leaders in the Postreform House* (Chicago: University of Chicago Press, 1991), and Sean Theriault, *Party Polarization in Congress* (New York: Cambridge University Press, 2008).

82 **did authorize the Speaker to resolve jurisdictional disputes:** Scott Adler, *Why Congressional Reforms Fail* (Chicago: University of Chicago Press, 2002).

83 **limited the use of presidential impoundment:** John J. Coleman, *Party Decline in America*, 69.

83 **would help the legislative branch compete with the president:** Philip A. Wallach, *Why Congress*, 112.

83 **Congressional Black Caucus was formed in 1971:** Susan Webb Hammond, *Congressional Caucuses in National Policymaking* (Baltimore: Johns Hopkins University Press, 1997).

84 **president's approval rating plummeted:** "A Pardon That Took a Decade to Forgive," Gallup, September 7, 2017.

85 **"improbable members of Congress":** Tip O'Neill with William Novak, *Man of the House:*

The Life and Political Memoirs of Speaker Tip O'Neill (New York: Random House, 1987), 283; Sanford J. Ungar, "Bleak House: Frustration on Capitol Hill," *Atlantic Monthly,* July 1977: 32.

85 **"I didn't think that Watergate would carry this far":** Jeffrey Alderman, "Watergate Spills Over Republicans," *Austin American Statesman,* November 6, 1974.

85 **"a large share of the burden for shaping the future":** Robert Shogan, "GOP Founders in Riptides of Watergate, Pardon, Economy," *Los Angeles Times,* November 6, 1974.

85 **change the way their party conducted business:** John Lawrence, *The Class of '74*.

85 **had run on traditional domestic issues:** John Lawrence, *The Class of '74*.

86 **slurring his words in front of a packed house of reporters:** Julian E. Zelizer, *On Capitol Hill,* 125–77.

87 **"there is a mood of reform in the air on Capitol Hill":** Julian E. Zelizer, *On Capitol Hill,* 163.

87 **"since George Norris knocked over 'Uncle Joe' Cannon in 1911":** Julian E. Zelizer, *On Capitol Hill,* 167.

88 **asked one member of the Steering Committee:** "Earthquake in the Congress," *Newsweek,* January 27, 1975: 27.

88 **had put his mistress, Elizabeth Ray, on the public payroll:** "A Whiff of Rebellion in the 94th," *Time,* January 27, 1975: 26.

89 **when three were deposed, they got the message:** Sidney Waldman, "Majority Leadership in the House of Representatives," *Political Science Quarterly* 95, no. 3 (Autumn 1980): 379.

89 **"they will be accountable to the Democratic Majority":** Julian E. Zelizer, *On Capitol Hill,* 170.

89 **"brings the seniority system crashing down":** Richard L. Lyons and Mary Russell, "Democrats Oust House Chairmen Hebert, Poage," *Washington Post,* January 17, 1975.

90 **Senate held only forty-nine votes to obtain cloture:** Ezra Klein, "The Definitive Case for Ending the Filibuster," Vox, October 1, 2020.

91 **votes on cloture swelled from six in 1969–1970 to twenty in 1971–1972:** Cloture Motions, U.S. Senate, Senate, https://www.senate.gov/legislative/cloture/clotureCounts.htm.

91 **closing down southern conservatives appeared to have become easier:** Julian E. Zelizer, *On Capitol Hill,* 172–73.

92 **"I don't have any strings on me":** John Dillin, "Carter Says

He Feels Solid U.S. Mandate," *Christian Science Monitor,* November 8, 1976.

92 **"how many Americans are listening to the debates which are made?":** Julia Jacobs, "As C-SPAN Turns 40, at Top Executive Reflects on Bringing Cameras to Congress," *New York Times,* March 19, 2019.

92 **broadcasting the House feed without journalistic commentary:** Stephen Frantzich and John Sullivan, *The C-SPAN Revolution* (Norman: University of Oklahoma Press, 1996).

93 **"amendment after amendment that didn't mean a damn":** John Lawrence, *The Class of '74,* 238.

93 **"when I am to fill out a form and the form says 'occupation'":** Samuel C. Patterson, "Party Leadership in the U.S. Senate," *Legislative Studies Quarterly* 14, no.3 (August 1989): 401, 405; Sidney Waldman, "Majority Leadership in the House of Representatives," 373–93.

94 **"The only way to score on this play":** Tip O'Neill with William Novak, *Man of the House*.

94 **Restrictive special rules clamped down on floor activity:** Philip A. Wallach, *Why Congress,* 126.

94–95 **O'Neill was more visible than any other member:** Douglas B. Harris, "The Rise of the Public Speakership," *Political Science Quarterly* 113, no. 2 (Summer 1998): 193–212.

95 **Wright iced out the GOP from deliberations:** John E. Owens, "The Return of Party Government in the U.S. House of Representatives: Central Leadership—Committee Relations in the 104th Congress," *British Journal of Political Science* 27, no. 2 (April 1997): 248–49; Barbara Sinclair, "The Emergence of Strong Leadership in the 1980s House of Representatives," *Journal of Politics* 54, no. 3 (August 1992): 657–84; David T. Canon, "The Institutionalization of Leadership in the U.S. Congress," *Legislative Studies Quarterly* 14, no. 3 (August 1989): 417.

95 **"He likes to go out and grab the nettles":** Susan F. Rasky, "Everyone Has Something to Say About Wright," *New York Times,* December 18, 1987.

95 **"this is the first time I've ever seen us readjust the sun":** Anne Swardson and Tom Kenworthy, "Wright Ekes Out Tax Bill's Passage," *Washington Post,* October 30, 1987. For a discussion of this debate in a broader context, see Julian E. Zelizer, *Burning Down the House: Newt Gingrich, the Fall of a Speaker, and the Rise of the New Republican Party* (New York:

Penguin Press, 2020), and John Barry, *The Ambition and the Power: The Fall of Jim Wright* (New York: Viking, 1989).

95 **"instead of gracefully acknowledging defeat, he cheats":** Eric Pianin, "House GOP's Frustrations Intensify," *Washington Post*, December 21, 1987.

96 **empowered Speakers to easily remove and replace:** Steve S. Smith, Jason M. Roberts, and Ryan J. Vander Wielen, *The American Congress*, 161.

96 **PACs became a key source of campaign funds:** Robert Boatright, "Campaign Finance Laws," in *Encyclopedia of American Political Parties and Elections,* updated ed., eds. Larry J. Sabato and Howard Ernst (New York: Facts on File, 2007), 55.

96 **campaign funds to loyal incumbents and challengers:** Damon Cann, "Political Action Committee, Leadership," in *Encyclopedia of American Political Parties and Elections*, 277.

96 **turned into major forces for raising funds and spending money on elections:** Mark D. Brewer and L. Sandy Maisel, *Parties and Elections in America,* 8th ed. (New York: Rowman & Littlefield, 2019), 170.

96 **there was literally a price to pay for crossing the party leadership:** Frances E. Lee, *Insecure Majorities: Congress and the Perpetual Campaign* (Chicago: University of Chicago Press, 2016), 78; Jacob Hacker and Paul Pierson, *Winner-Take-All-Politics: How Washington Made the Rich Richer* (New York: Simon & Schuster, 2010), 1; Sorauf, "Power, Money, and Responsibility in the Major American Parties," in *Responsible Partisanship?*, 91–92.

97 **much greater outreach to small contributors:** Paul S. Herrnson, *Party Campaigning in the 1980s* (Cambridge, MA: Harvard University Press, 1988), 31–38. See also David Adamany, "Political Parties in the 1980s," in *Money and Politics in the United States Financing of Elections in the 1980s,* ed. Michael J. Malbin (Chatham, NJ: Chatham House Publishers, 1984), 70–121.

97 **hired a press secretary:** Frances E. Lee, *Insecure Majorities,* 89.

97 **the ability of old loci of power:** C. Lawrence Evans and Walter J. Oleszek, "The Procedural Context of Senate Deliberation," in *Esteemed Colleagues: Civility and Deliberation in the U.S. Senate,* ed. Burdett A. Loomis (Washington: Brookings, 2000), 9.

98 **strong partisan leadership was conditional:** David W. Rohde, *Parties and Leaders in the Postreform House.*

98 **"parties' ability to assert themselves is limited":** Roger H. Davidson, "Representation and Congressional Committees," *Annals of the American Academy of Political and Social Science* 411 (January 1974): 59–60.

98 **split-ticket voting as a share of ballots cast:** Roger H. Davidson, Walter J. Oleszek, Frances E. Lee, and Eric Schickler, *Congress and Its Members*, 89.

99 **capitalized on opposition to the civil rights revolution:** Earl and Merle Black, *Politics and Society in the South* (Cambridge, MA: Harvard University Press, 1987).

99 **"when we can get the electoral votes of eleven Southern states?":** Sam Tanenhaus, "Original Sin," *New Republic*, February 10, 2023.

100 **lent support to increasingly hard-line positions on race:** Matthew Lassiter, *The Silent Majority: Suburban Politics in the Sunbelt South* (Princeton, NJ: Princeton University Press, 2006).

100 **"It was a realignment of massive proportions":** Warren E. Miller, "Party Identification, Realignment, and Party Voting: Back to the Basics," *American Political Science Review* 85, no. 2 (June 1991): 562.

100 **And the numbers kept growing:** Earl Black and Merle Black, *The Rise of Southern Republicans* (Cambridge, MA: The Belknap Press of Harvard University Press, 2002), 222.

100 **wealthier states with cutting-edge industry veered Democratic:** Andrew Gellman, *Red State, Blue State, Rich State, Poor State: Why Americans Vote the Way They Do* (Princeton, NJ: Princeton University Press, 2008).

100 **believed that economic development was a result of low-tax, anti-union policies:** Nelson Polsby, *How Congress Evolves: Social Bases of Institutional Change* (New York: Oxford University Press, 2005). Political scientists have vigorously debated how much voters naturally divided and how much of the division was being driven by elites. For an example, see Morris Fiorina, *Culture War? The Myth of a Polarized America*, 3rd ed. (New York: Longman, 2010), and Alan I. Abramowitz, *The Disappearing Center: Engaged Citizens, Polarization, and American Democracy* (New Haven, CT: Yale University Press, 2010).

101 **appealing on an economic, not just ideological, level:** Bruce Schulman, *From Cotton Belt to Sunbelt: Federal Policy, Economic Development, and the Transformation of the South,*

1938–1970 (New York: Oxford University Press, 1991).

101 **made the party seem safe to their personal bottom line:** Lily Geismer, *Don't Blame Us: Suburban Liberals and the Transformation of the Democratic Party* (Princeton, NJ: Princeton University Press, 2014).

102 **was successful in only four counties:** Drew Desilver, "The Growing Domination of the Nation's Largest Counties," Pew Research, July 21, 2016.

102 **northeastern conservatives who no longer felt comfortable in the GOP:** Lily Geismer, *Left Behind: The Democrats' Failed Attempt to Solve Inequality* (New York: Basic Books, 2023); Nelson Lichtenstein and Judith Stein, *A Fabulous Failure: The Clinton Presidency and the Transformation of American Capitalism* (Princeton, NJ: Princeton University Press, 2023).

102 **the impact of government planning and intervention:** Lilliana Mason, *Uncivil Agreement: How Politics Became Our Identity* (Chicago: University of Chicago Press, 2018).

102 **"landslide counties":** William A. Galston and Pietro S. Nivola, "Vote Like Thy Neighbor: Political Polarization and Sorting," *Brookings Commentary,* May 11, 2008.

102 **sorting of voters, which accelerated fivefold:** Ethan Kaplan, Jörg L. Spenkuch, and Rebecca Sullivan, "Partisan Spatial Sorting in the United States: A Theoretical and Empirical Overview," *Journal of Public Economics* 211 (July 2022); Corey Lang and Shanna Pearson-Merkowitz, "Partisan Sorting Is a Very Recent Phenomenon and Has Been Driven by the Southern Realignment," *London School of Economics Blog,* November 10, 2015.

102 **were more attracted to areas that felt comfortable politically:** Bill Bishop, *The Big Sort: Why the Clustering of Like-Minded America Is Tearing Us Apart* (Boston: Houghton Mifflin, 2008).

103 **elements of popular culture that reflected their points of view:** Ezra Klein, *Why We're Polarized* (New York: Simon & Schuster, 2020).

103 **parties were dead was turning out to be dead wrong:** Larry M. Bartels, "Partisanship and Voting Behavior, 1952–1996," *American Journal of Political Science,* 44, no.1 (January 2000): 35.

104 **"divided government in their experience had been infrequent and short-lived":** James Sundquist, "Needed: A Political Theory for the New Era of Coalition Government in the United States," *Political Science*

Quarterly 103, no. 4 (Winter 1988–1989), 614, 626.

104 **divided government still had the capacity:** David Mayhew, *Divided We Govern: Party Control, Lawmaking, and Investigations 1946–1990* (New Haven, CT: Yale University Press, 1988). Critics of Mayhew note that he doesn't do enough to distinguish different kinds of legislation and what sorts of bills never make it onto the agenda under divided government. See Steven S. Smith, "Review: Divided We Govern," University of Minnesota Law School, Law Commons, 1992.

104 **increased the number of presidential vetoes:** Steve S. Smith, Jason M. Roberts, and Ryan J. Vander Wielen, *The American Congress,* 317.

104 **The percentage fell when power was divided:** Roger H. Davidson, Walter J. Oleszek, Frances E. Lee, and Eric Schickler, *Congress and Its Members,* 285.

105 **was almost always higher when one party controlled:** R. Douglas Arnold, "Explaining Legislative Achievements" in *Congress and Policymaking in the 21st Century,* eds. Jeffrey A. Jenkins and Eric M. Patashnik (New York: Cambridge University Press, 2016), 309–10.

CHAPTER FOUR

106 **into dens of toxic, dysfunctional blood sport:** For a sharp critique of the notion that polarization in current times is nearly as bad as the nineteenth century, see David R. Mayhew, *The Imprint of Congress* (New Haven, CT: Yale University Press, 2017).

107 **now even being deployed for personal vendettas:** Barbara Sinclair, "Individualism, Partisanship, and Cooperation in the Senate," in Burdett A. Loomis, ed. *Esteemed Colleagues: Civility and Deliberation in the U.S. Senate.*

107 **filibuster heightened the partisan incentives:** Sean M. Theriault and Mickey Edwards, *Congress: The First Branch,* 272.

107 **became a permanent buttress for super-majoritarian requirements:** Catherine Fiske and Erwin Chemerinsky, "The Filibuster," *Stanford Law Review* 49, no. 2 (January 1997): 181–254. See also Keith Krehbiel, *Pivotal Politics: A Theory of U.S. Lawmaking* (Chicago: University of Chicago Press, 1998).

107 **compared to six in 1969–1970:** Cloture Motions, U.S. Senate, https://www.senate.gov/legislative/cloture/clotureCounts.htm.

108 **wealthy and powerful minorities benefit disproportionally:** Melissa

Schwartzberg, *Counting the Many: The Origins and Limits of Supermajority Rule* (New York: Cambridge University Press, 2014).

108 **either appointing their own loyalists:** Sean M. Theriault and Mickey Edwards, *Congress: The First Branch,* 199–200.

108 **apprenticeship and collegial reciprocity disappeared:** Eric M. Uslaner, *The Decline of Comity in Congress* (Ann Arbor: University of Michigan Press, 1993), 33–38; Burdett A. Loomis, ed. *Esteemed Colleagues.*

108 **Threatening impeachment became more commonplace:** Gregory Downs, "Impeachment After Trump," in *The Presidency of Donald J. Trump,* ed. Julian E. Zelizer (Princeton, NJ: Princeton University Press, 2022), 358–59.

109 **"directing attention away from the tensions or conflicts":** Eric M. Patashnik, *Countermobilization: Policy Feedback and Backlash in a Polarized Age* (Chicago: University of Chicago Press, 2023), 29–30.

109 **final votes more frequently fell along party lines:** Drew Desilver, "Up Until the Postwar Era, U.S. Supreme Court Confirmations Usually Were Routine Business," Pew Research Center, February 7, 2022; Sarah A. Binder and Forrest Maltzman, "Senatorial Delay in Confirming Federal Judges, 1947–1998," *American Journal of Political Science* 46, no.1 (January 2022): 190–91.

109 **an integral component of political fault lines:** Charles M. Cameron and Jonathan P. Kastellec, *Making the Supreme Court: The Politics of Appointments, 1930–2020* (New York: Oxford University Press, 2023).

109 **refused to hold hearings for more than fifty:** Helen Dewar, "Polarized Politics, Confirmation Process," *Washington Post,* May 11, 2003.

109 **blocked a historically high level of judicial nominees:** Steven Levitsky and Daniel Ziblatt, *How Democracies Die,* 152.

110 **"limit Congress's capacity for more than lowest common denominator deals":** Sarah Binder, "Polarized We Govern?" Brookings Center for Effective Public Management, 2014.

111 **documented how Democrats and Republicans polarized in different ways:** Thomas Mann and Norman J. Ornstein, *It's Even Worse Than It Looks: How the American Constitutional System Collided with the New Politics of Extremism* (New York: Basic Books, 2012); Matt Grossman and David A. Hopkins, *Asymmetric Politics: Ideological Republicans and Group Interest*

Democrats (New York: Oxford University Press, 2016), 3.

111 **allowed them to serve as gatekeepers:** Steven Levitsky and Daniel Ziblatt, *How Democracies Die*, 96–118.

112 **"helps you to govern but it collapses your majority":** Matthew N. Green and Jeffrey Crouch, *Newt Gingrich: The Rise and Fall of a Party Entrepreneur* (Lawrence, KS: University Press of Kansas, 2022), 33.

112 **"willing to stand up in . . . a slugfest":** "A 1978 Speech by Gingrich," *Frontline.*

113 **"a capacity for outrage that the older Republicans seemed to lack":** Tom DeLay with Stephen Mansfield, *No Retreat, No Surrender: One American's Fight* (New York: Sentinel, 2007), 78.

114 **"You deliberately stood in that well before an empty House":** T. R. Reid, "It's 'Tip's Greatest Hits,' Electrifying a Closed House GOP Circuit," *Washington Post,* May 29, 1984.

115 **"that becomes the mesmerizing event that people remember you by":** Myra MacPherson, "Newt Gingrich, Point Man in a House Divided," *Washington Post,* June 12, 1989.

115 **"Congress is a smash hit on C-SPAN":** Sandy Grady, "Tip's 'Gong Show,'" *Philadelphia Daily News,* May 17, 1984.

116 **"must resolve to bring this period of mindless cannibalism to an end!":** Speaker Jim Wright, "Resignation Speech," May 31, 1989, https://www.americanrhetoric.com/speeches/jimwrightresignation.htm.

116 **featured words such as "treasonous," "pathetic," and "anti-child":** GOPAC, "Language a Key Mechanism of Control," 1990. For the full story of Gingrich in the 1980s, see Julian E. Zelizer, *Burning Down the House.*

116 **"Newt was willing to tear up the system to get the majority":** Sheryl Gay Stolberg, "Gingrich Stuck to Caustic Path in Ethics Battles," *New York Times,* January 26, 2012.

117 **"He was a kind of McCarthyite who succeeded":** Cited in Steven Levitsky and Daniel Ziblatt, *How Democracies Die*, 149.

117 **"I think it is nonsense to sell out to the Democrats":** William J. Eaton, "Gingrich Sends Warning on Budget," *Los Angeles Times,* July 30, 1990.

117 **"would have destroyed my effectiveness":** Julian E. Zelizer, "Seizing Power: Conservatives and Congress Since the 1970s," in *The New American Polity: Activist Government, the Redefinition of*

Citizenship, and Conservative Mobilization, eds. Theda Skocpol and Paul Pierson (Princeton, NJ: Princeton University Press, 2007), 123.

118 **several freshmen to seats on five major committees:** Linda Killian, *The Freshmen: What Happened to the Republican Revolution?* (New York: Westview, 1998), 75–76.

118 **term-limited all committee chairs to six years:** Linda Killian, *The Freshmen,* 75–76.

118 **granting his office full control over making the determination:** Roger H. Davidson, Walter J. Oleszek, Frances E. Lee, and Eric Schickler, *Congress and Its Members,* 202.

119 **authorized unlimited donations to local and state party-building activities:** Stephen Ansolabehere and James M. Snyder Jr., "Soft Money, Hard Money, Strong Parties," *Columbia Law Review* 100, no. 3 (April 2000): 599. See also Nolan McCarty and Eric Schickler, "On the Theory of Parties," *Annual Review of Political Science* 21 (2018): 175–93.

119 **"both parties now use soft money for Congressional":** Jane F. Roberts, "States and Localities in 1983: Recession, Reform, Renewal," *Intergovernmental Perspective* 10, no. 1 (Winter 1984): 17; Elizabeth Drew, *Politics and Money: The New Road to Corruption* (New York: MacMillan, 1983).

119 **emerged as the giants in the room:** Thomas E. Mann and Anthony Corrado, "Party Polarization and Campaign Finance," Brookings Center for Effective Public Management, July 2014.

119 **the rudimentary system that had previously existed:** Robert Caro, *The Years of Lyndon Johnson: Means of Ascent* (New York: Knopf, 1982).

120 **took a pro forma vote to raise the debt ceiling:** H. J. Cooke and M. Katzen, "The Public Debt Limit," *Journal of Finance* 9, no. 3 (September 1954): 298–303; U.S. Government Accountability Office, "Debt Limit," 2023; Glenn Kessler, "The Truth About the National Debt Ceiling," *Washington Post,* May 3, 2003.

121 **Republicans would let the nation suffer the dire economic consequences:** David E. Sanger, "Gingrich Threatens U.S. Default If Clinton Won't Bend on Budget," *New York Times,* September 22, 1995.

121 **to impeach President Clinton for having perjured himself:** Steve Kornacki, *The Red and the Blue: The 1990s and the Birth of Political Tribalism* (New York: Ecco, 2018).

122 **had been secretly negotiating with Clinton:** Steve Gillon, *The Pact: Bill Clinton, Newt Gingrich, and the Rivalry That Defined a Generation* (New York: Oxford University Press, 2008).

122 **allied with Democrats to secure additional funds for veterans:** Steve S. Smith, Jason M. Roberts, and Ryan J. Vander Wielen, *The American Congress,* 151; Roger H. Davidson, Walter J. Oleszek, Frances E. Lee, and Eric Schickler, *Congress and Its Members,* 144.

122–123 **pushed through a rules change just to protect Majority Leader Tom DeLay:** Paul Blumenthal, "Dennis Hastert's History as Speaker," The Sunlight Foundation, October 3, 2006.

123 **"especially from the perspective of a political conservative":** Tom DeLay, "Farewell Address to House of Representatives," June 8, 2006.

124 **"retrench and sabotage significant portions of the federal bureaucracy":** William Howell and Terry Moe, "The Strongman Presidency and the Two Logics of Presidential Power," *Presidential Studies Quarterly* 53 (2023): 164–65.

125 **"era of big government is over":** Nolan McCarty, *Polarization: What Everyone Needs to Know* (New York: Oxford University Press, 2019), 43.

125 **remained more wedded to traditional norms of governance:** Michael Kazin, *What It Took to Win: A History of the Democratic Party* (New York: Farrar, Straus and Giroux, 2022); Lizabeth Cohen, *Making a New Deal: Industrial Workers in Chicago, 1919–1939* (New York: Cambridge University Press, 2008).

125 **tie up the machinery of government:** Nolan McCarty, "The Policy Effects of Political Polarization," in *The Transformation of American Politics,* 223–55.

125 **so ideologically driven that they preferred to avoid the party:** Raymond J. La Raja and Brian F. Schaffner, *Campaign Finance and Political Polarization: When Purists Prevail* (Ann Arbor: University of Michigan Press, 2015), 37–119.

126 **genuinely believed market-based solutions to perennial policy problems:** Lily Geismer, *Left Behind.*

126 **felt that they had nowhere to turn:** On the mobilization of business in Washington, see Hacker and Pierson, *Winner-Take-All-Politics*; Benjamin C. Waterhouse, *Lobbying America: The Politics of Business from Nixon to NAFTA* (Princeton, NJ: Princeton University Press, 2013). On the "neoliberal" consensus, see Gary Gerstle, *The Rise and Fall of the Neoliberal Order: America and the World in the Free Market* (New York:

Oxford University Press, 2022). This was also true with drug policy. See Matthew Lassiter, *The Suburban Crisis: White America and the War on Drugs* (Princeton, NJ: Princeton University Press, 2023); Nicholas Carnes, "Who Votes for Inequality," in *Congress and Policymaking in the 21st Century*, 106–33.

127 **"came from those House members who came to the Senate":** Sean Theriault, *The Gingrich Senators: The Roots of Partisan Warfare in Congress* (New York: Oxford University Press, 2013), 202.

128 **partisan divisions were nearly even in most of the twenty-first century:** Katherine Schaeffer, "Slim Majorities Have Become More Common in the U.S. Senate and House," Pew Research Center, December 1, 2020.

129 **"has suffered from the defeatism that characterized Republicans":** Frances E. Lee, *Insecure Majorities*.

130 **after 1988, the GOP chose confrontation:** Frances E. Lee, *Insecure Majorities*, 53, 100–105, 112–41.

130 **independents voted regularly for one party or the other:** Ezra Klein, "Blame the Polls. . . ." *The American Prospect*, September 20, 2006.

131 **could be to anger valuable pockets of Americans:** Bill Bishop, *The Big Sort*, 195.

131 **raised and directed resources to party building:** Daniel J. Galvin, *Presidential Party Building: Dwight D. Eisenhower to George W. Bush* (Princeton, NJ: Princeton University Press, 2009); Charles Cameron, "Studying the Polarized Presidency," *Presidential Studies Quarterly* 32. no. 4 (December 2002): 647–63.

131 **"I'm not willing to preside over people who are cannibals":** "Excerpts from Phone Call About Gingrich's Future," *New York Times*, November 8, 1998.

132 **"without stopping to realize the flames are going to consume his own apartment":** Allen Myerson, "From One Fallen Speaker to Another," *New York Times*, November 12, 1998.

132 **fueled and magnified by the institutions that surrounded it:** Kevin Kruse and Julian E. Zelizer, *Fault Lines: A History of the United States Since 1974* (New York: W. W. Norton & Company, 2019).

133 **party committees tried to coordinate their efforts with these groups:** Michael M. Franz, "Interest Groups in Electoral Politics: 2012 in Context," *The Forum* 10, no. 4 (2012): 69; Jeff Smith and David C. Kimball, "Barking Louder: Interest

Groups in the 2012 Election," *The Forum* 10, no. 4 (2012): 85–86.

133 **moved "money from accountable actors, the political parties, to unaccountable groups":** Thomas B. Edsall, "Small Donors Are a Big Problem," *New York Times*, August 30, 2023.

133 **would support or oppose the nominees:** Charles M. Cameron and Jonathan P. Kastellec, *Making the Supreme Court*, 118.

134 **"What use is a Republican to us, if all they do is vote with Democrats?":** "What Exactly Is the Tea Party," BBC.com, September 16, 2010.

135 **"less predictable than what we previously believed":** Charles Riley, "S&P Downgrades U.S. Rating," CNN.com, August 6, 2011.

135 **"it's a hostage that's worth ransoming":** David A. Farenthold, Lori Montgomery, and Paul Kane, "In Debt Deal, the Triumph of the Old Washington," *Washington Post*, August 3, 2011.

137 **"irreparable harm to the institution":** "John Boehner, House Speaker, Will Resign from Office," *New York Times*, September 25, 2015.

137 **later admitted that he had been dealing with "legislative terrorists":** "Former House Speaker John Boehner Accuses Some in Congress of Being 'Political Terrorists,'" *CBS Sunday Morning*, April 9, 2021.

138 **embraced the polarization of the judicial nomination and confirmation process:** Richard L. Hansen, "Polarization and the Judiciary," *Annual Review of Political Science* 22 (May 2019): 261–76.

138 **fewer committee hearings or courtesy meetings for nominees:** Mark E. Owens, "Changing Senate Norms: Judicial Confirmations in a Nuclear Age," *PS: Political Science & Politics* 51, no. 1 (January 2018): 119–23.

138 **"We create an inventory of losses":** Alex MacGillis, *The Cynic: The Political Education of Mitch McConnell* (New York: Simon & Schuster, 2014), 97–98.

138 **ongoing efforts to fill the federal courts:** Julian E. Zelizer, "McConnell's President: The Anti-Institutionalist Presidency," in *Disruption? The Senate During the Trump Era*, ed. Sean M. Theriault (New York: Oxford University Press, 2024), 148-66.

138 **the loosely organized Tea Party got from Fox News:** Vanessa Williamson, Theda Skocpol, and John Coggin, "The Tea Party and the Remaking of American Conservatism," *Perspectives on Politics* 9, no. 1 (March 2011): 29.

139 **"it has forced the Democrat-Media Complex to finally play**

some defense": Andrew Breitbart, *Righteous Indignation: Excuse Me While I Save the World* (New York: Grand Central Publishing, 2020), 211.

139 **Conspiratorial rumors gained much more traction in right-wing information streams:** Adam J. Berinsky, *Political Rumors: Why We Accept Misinformation and How to Fight It* (Princeton, NJ: Princeton University Press, 2023); "Political Polarization and Media Habits," Pew Research Center, October 21, 2014.

140 ***"Let's make it where you can bite ears":*** Emily Nussbaum, "Country Music's Culture Wars and the Remaking of Nashville," *New Yorker,* July 17, 2023.

140 **Trump and the congressional GOP worked closely together:** Roger H. Davidson, Walter J. Oleszek, Frances E. Lee, and Eric Schickler, *Congress and Its Members*, 283.

141 **"impeachment talk" has become normalized:** Gregory Downs, "Impeachments After Trump," 358.

141 **being censured has become a badge of honor:** Carl Hulse, "Once Rare, Impeachments and Censures Have Become the Norm in Congress," *New York Times,* August 8, 2023.

142 **Persuasion was less relevant than mobilization:** John Sides, Chris Tausanovitch, and Lynn Vavreck, *The Bitter End: The 2020 Presidential Campaign and the Challenge to American Democracy* (Princeton, NJ: Princeton University Press, 2022).

142 **"do not understand how their opponents can possibly understand the world as they do":** Thomas B. Edsall, "'Gut-Level Hatred' Is Consuming Our Political Life," *New York Times,* July 19, 2023.

143 **Affective partisanship:** Lilliana Mason, *Uncivil Agreement: How Politics Became Our Identity* (Chicago: University of Chicago Press, 2018).

143 **"a struggle for the very soul of America itself":** President Joe Biden, "Remarks by President Biden on Standing Up for American Democracy," November 3, 2022.

144 **Jimmy Kimmel:** Trish Bendix, "Late Night Hosts Razz Republicans Trying to Oust Mike Johnson," *New York Times,* April 19, 2024; Tara Suter, "Greene Says She Doesn't Care If 'Speaker's Office Becomes a Revolving Door,'" *The Hill,* April 18, 2024.

144 **"You can't govern by shooting yourself":** "'You Can't Govern Yourself by Shooting Yourself in the Head Every Day':

Newt Gingrich Offers Advice for How Mike Johnson Can Stay Speaker," *Politico Magazine*, April 19, 2024.

CHAPTER FIVE

146 **Hyperpartisanship is destructive:** Ronald Brownstein, *The Second Civil War: How Extreme Partisanship Has Paralyzed Washington and Polarized America* (New York: Penguin, 2007).

147 **would empower leaders to make tough decisions while being checked from abusing power:** Frances McCall Rosenbluth and Ian Shapiro, *Responsible Parties*, 5.

148 **responsible partisanship expands the range of opportunities:** Critics of Mayhew have pointed out that Mayhew doesn't pay attention to legislation that was not passed as a result of divided government or doesn't grapple with the aggressiveness of the legislation he measures. See Steven S. Smith, "Review: Divided We Govern," University of Minnesota Law School, Law Commons, 1992.

148 **has vastly diminished the odds for major legislation:** Barbara Sinclair, "Partisan Polarization and Congressional Policymaking," and Craig Volden and Alan E. Wiseman, "Entrepreneurial Politics, Policy Gridlock, and Legislative Effectiveness" in *Congress and Policymaking in the 21st Century*, 21–72.

148 **they need choices within the political system to express their disagreement:** Alan I. Abramowitz, *The Great Alignment: Race, Party Transformation, and the Rise of Donald Trump* (New Haven, CT: Yale University Press, 2018).

149 **"he sure has exacerbated the shocks":** Ronald Brownstein, "Why the U.S. 'Does Not Get to Assume That It Lasts Forever,'" *New York Times*, July 4, 2023.

149 **Congress still has shown the capacity to deal with:** Philip A. Wallach, *Why Congress*, 171.

150 **can generate countervailing pressure to the hyperpartisan imperative:** Russell Berman, "A Radical Idea for Fixing Polarization," *The Atlantic*, July 6, 2023.

150 **entrenched anti-majoritarian power of the Electoral College and the Senate:** Jill Lepore, "How to Stave Off Constitutional Extinction," *New York Times*, July 2, 2023; Steven Levitsky and Daniel Ziblatt, "End Minority Rule," *New York Times*, October 23, 2020.

150 **can test alternatives against the demanding criterion of political acceptability:** Nelson W. Polsby, "Legislatures," in *Handbook of Political Science:*

Governmental Institutions and Processes, eds. Fred I. Greenstein and Nelson W. Polsby (Reading, MA: Addison-Wesley, 1975), 303.

152 **"Bickering over the debt ceiling is a waste of time and energy":** Louise Sheiner, "Why Congress Needs to Abolish the Debt Limit: Testimony Before the House Budget Committee," Brookings, February 22, 2022.

152 **"the 'deemed authority' to raise the debt ceiling automatically":** Willem E. Buiter, "Eliminate the Debt Ceiling," *Project Syndicate*, January 31, 2023.

152 **"eliminate the debt limit entirely":** Robert Rubin, "Get Rid of the Debt Ceiling Once and For All," *The Atlantic*, June 5, 2023.

153 **debt ceiling could also be raised through the reconciliation process:** Dylan Matthews, "Abolish the Debt Ceiling," Vox, February 10, 2021; Megan S. Lynch and James V. Saturno, "The Budget Reconciliation Process and the Statutory Limit on the Debt," Congressional Research Service, November 8, 2022.

153 **from even trying to tackle many crucial problems:** Ezra Klein, "The Definitive Case for Ending the Filibuster," Vox, October 1, 2020.

153 **"is a tool to preserve the status quo and make it harder to change":** Adam Jentleson, *Kill Switch: The Rise of the Modern Senate and the Crippling of Democracy* (New York: Liveright, 2021).

154 **has little reason to cooperate with the majority:** Keith Krehbiel, *Pivotal Politics: A Theory of U.S. Lawmaking* (Chicago: University of Chicago Press, 1998); Eric Schickler and Greg Wawro, *Filibuster: Obstruction and Lawmaking in the United States Senate* (Princeton, NJ: Princeton University Press, 2006).

154 **trying to understand who is to blame for their problems going unsolved:** Ezra Klein, "The Definitive Case for Ending the Filibuster."

155 **which has become the main "majoritarian exception":** Congressional Research Service, "The Budget Reconciliation Process: Timing of Legislative Action," 2016; Molly Reynolds, *Exceptions to the Rule: The Politics of Filibuster Limitations in the U.S. Senate* (Washington, D.C.: Brookings Institution Press, 2017).

155 **Gimmicks are used to squeeze as much as possible into this process:** Ezra Klein, "The Senate Has Become a Dadaist Nightmare," *New York Times*, February 4, 2021.

156 **by allowing a greater range of appointments to circumvent the committees:** Max Stier, "The

Senate Confirmation Process Is Broken. Here's How We Can Fix It," *Washington Post,* August 17, 2023.

156 **to raise enough so that they can donate unused funds:** Michael S. Kang, "Hyperpartisan Campaign Finance," *Emory Law Journal* 7, no. 5 (2021): 1188, 1191.

156 **in what they refer to as "call time":** Eric Alterman, *Kabuki Democracy,* 123; Ryan Grim and Sabrina Siddiqui, "Call Time for Congress Shows How Fundraising Dominates Bleak Work Life," *Huffington Post,* January 8, 2013.

157 **improves the quality of political parties as institutions connecting voters:** Ian Vandenwalker and Daniel I. Weiner, *Stronger Democracy: Rethinking Reform* (New York: Brennan Center of Justice, 2015).

158 **ensure that the concerns and preferences of ordinary voters carry at least some weight:** Mark Schmitt, "What If You Had As Much Political Influence as a Billionaire," CNN.com, February 16, 2015.

158 **those who donate tend to be among the most ideologically extreme:** Michael J. Barber, "Ideological Donors, Contribution Limits, and the Polarization of American Legislatures," *Journal of Politics* 78, no. 1 (2016): 296–310; Richard H. Pildes, "Small-Donor-Based Campaign-Finance Reform and Political Polarization," *Yale Law Journal Reform* 129 (2019): 149–70. For a useful review of this literature, see Thomas B. Edsall, "Small Donors Are a Big Problem."

158 **several reforms that aim to reinvigorate parties in campaigns:** Raymond J. La Raja and Brian F. Schaffner, *Campaign Finance and Political Polarization: When Purists Prevail* (Ann Arbor: University of Michigan Press, 2015).

159 **"a systematic, step-by-step lawmaking process":** Congressional Research Service, "The 'Regular Order': A Perspective," November 6, 2020.

161 **willing to enforce regular order and promote related norms:** Matthew Green and Daniel Burns, "What Might Bring Regular Order Back to the House," *PS: Political Science and Politics,* April 2010, 225.

162 **"weak parties and strong partisanship":** Julia Azari, "Weak Parties and Strong Partisanship Are a Bad Combination," Vox, November 3, 2016.

162 **"are unrooted in communities and unfelt":** For an excellent, detailed history of the parties and partisanship, see Daniel Schlozman and Sam Rosenfeld, *The Hollow Parties: The Many Pasts and Disordered Present of American Party Politics* (Princeton, NJ: Princeton University Press, 2024).

163 **and have submitted recommendations to congresspersons:** Commission on the Practice of Democratic Citizenship, *Our Common Purpose,* 2023.

163 **clear capacity to forge meaningful connections with frustrated voters:** Theda Skocpol and Vanessa Williamson, *The Tea Party and the Remaking of Republican Conservatism* (New York: Oxford University Press, 2012), and Theda Skocpol and Laura Putnam, "Women Are Rebuilding the Democratic Party from the Ground Up," *New Republic,* August 21, 2018.

164 **"Parties were stronger where they canvassed door-to-door":** Tabatha El-Haj and Didi Kuo, "Associational Party-Building," *Columbia Law Review* 122, no. 7 (November 2022): 127–76.

165 **Despite the fact that the population has more than doubled since that time:** Steve S. Smith, Jason M. Roberts, and Ryan J. Vander Wielen, *The American Congress,* 24.

165 **the most active and the most vocal persons in their specific electorate:** Danielle Allen, "Can the Capitol Hold a Much Bigger House? Yes, Here's How It Would Work," *Washington Post,* May 2, 2023. See also Larry Sabato, "Expand the House of Representatives," *Democracy* 8 (Spring 2008); Editors, "America Needs a Bigger House," *New York Times,* November 15, 2018; Mac Bower, "When It Comes to the House, Bigger Might Be Better," Democracy Docket, February 11, 2022; Lee Drutman, Jonathan D. Cohen, Yuval Levin, and Norman J. Ornstein, "The Case for Enlarging the House of Representatives," American Academy for Arts and Sciences, 2021.

166 **"will reduce the advantage of small states to an appropriate level":** Danielle Allen, "Our Democracy Is Menaced by Two Dragons. Here's How to Slay Them," *Washington Post,* July 20, 2023.

166 **to renovate the physical infrastructure of the House and adjacent office buildings:** Danielle Allen, "Can the Capitol Hold a Much Bigger House? Yes, Here's How It Would Work." See also Larry Sabato, "Expand the House of Representatives"; Editors, "America Needs a Bigger House"; Mac Bower, "When It Comes to the House, Bigger Might Be Better"; Lee Drutman, Jonathan D. Cohen, Yuval Levin, and Norman J. Ornstein, "The Case for Enlarging the House of Representatives."

166 **the results have been violence and chaos:** Joanne Freeman, *The Field of Blood: Violence in Congress and the Road to Civil War* (New York: Farrar, Straus and Giroux, 2018).

167 **"though insufficient attention to means can corrupt the ends":** James MacGregor Burns, *Leadership*, revised ed. (New York: Harper Perennial Classics, 2010)

168 **need to learn how to "disagree better":** Dan Baltz, "Utah Gov. Spencer Cox Wants Americans to Learn to 'Disagree Better,'" *Washington Post*, July 22, 2023.

168 **If more politicians would refuse to spread and reject disinformation:** Adam J. Berinsky *Political Rumors*.

169 **discussing, debating, refining, and testing proposals for reform:** Nelson Polsby, *Political Innovation in America: The Politics of Policy Initiation* (New Haven, CT: Yale University Press, 1984).

170 **grades the health of democracies:** Steven Levitsky and Daniel Ziblatt, "How American Democracy Fell So Far Behind," *The Atlantic*, September 5, 2023.

Columbia Global Reports is a nonprofit publishing imprint from Columbia University that commissions authors to produce works of original thinking and on-site reporting from all over the world, on a wide range of topics. Our books are short—novella-length, and readable in a few hours—but ambitious. They offer new ways of looking at and understanding the major issues of our time. Most readers are curious and busy. Our books are for them.

If this book changed the way you look at the world, and if you would like to support our mission, consider making a gift to help us share new ideas and stories.

Visit globalreports.columbia.edu to support our upcoming books, subscribe to our newsletter, and learn more. Thank you for being part of our community of readers and supporters.

Why Flying Is Miserable and How to Fix It
Ganesh Sitaraman

Putin's Exiles: Their Fight for a Better Russia
Paul Starobin

The Lie Detectives: In Search of a Playbook for Winning Elections in the Disinformation Age
Sasha Issenberg

Soul by Soul: The Evangelical Mission to Spread the Gospel to Muslims
Adriana Carranca

Climate Radicals: Why Our Environmental Politics Isn't Working
Cameron Abadi

Left Adrift: What Happened to Liberal Politics
Timothy Shenk